WHAT
it MEANS *to*
PRAY THROUGH

WHAT
it MEANS *to*
PRAY THROUGH

Mother Elizabeth Juanita Dabney

iUniverse, Inc.
Bloomington

What It Means To Pray Through

iUniverse books may be ordered through booksellers or by contacting:

iUniverse
1663 Liberty Drive
Bloomington, IN 47403
www.iuniverse.com
1-800-Authors (1-800-288-4677)

Because of the dynamic nature of the Internet, any web addresses or links contained in this book may have changed since publication and may no longer be valid. The views expressed in this work are solely those of the author and do not necessarily reflect the views of the publisher, and the publisher hereby disclaims any responsibility for them.

Any people depicted in stock imagery provided by Thinkstock are models, and such images are being used for illustrative purposes only.
Certain stock imagery © Thinkstock.

ISBN: 978-1-4759-2248-6 (sc)
ISBN: 978-1-4759-2249-3 (hc)
ISBN: 978-1-4759-2250-9 (ebk)

Printed in the United States of America

iUniverse rev. date: 05/22/2012

CONTENTS

I.   The Family Altar 1
II.   The Dark Days 8
III.   Angels Guard The Highway 15
IV.   A Vision Of The Future 22
V.   My Covenant Ends 27
VI.   God's Approval And Manifestation 33
VII.   California Trip Ends 40
VIII.   A New Day Dawns 43
IX.   The Golden Treasure 47
X.   Material For The Palace 52
XI.   Wisdom In The Prayer Cabinet 55
XII.   The Old Fashion Church Prayer Revival 63
XIII.   A Peep Into The Revival Scenes 69
XIV.   The House Of The Lord 73
XV.   Saved For The Purpose 75
XVI.   His Prayer Life Influenced Me 78
XVII.   Healing Testimonies 81

This Book is Dedicated

To My Sister

Mrs. Dorothy Brown

Who Helped Me in My Early

Christian Training

And

To My Son

John H. Dabney

Chapter I

The Family Altar

Since early childhood, a family altar has existed in my home. I know very little of my father because he died when I was young. However, my mother, who was a noted missionary, a gifted singer, and a great woman of prayer, kept me aware of the goodness of the family altar.

Doubtlessly, some will ask about the construction of the family altar. Is it material-something which is concrete and movable, or is it invisible and abstract? Indeed, the altar is more or less an intangible thing. It is a treaty, promise, or covenant between God and an individual to meet at a definite place at a definite time. At this meeting the individual thanks the Almighty for past blessings, and requests future favors. Likewise the Father admonishes and gives instructions.

The battle-weary Christian drags his tired body to the family altar after each encounter with the enemy. Sometimes, victory has been costly, but he is able to come to the family altar, and tell the Father that he has made another day's journey.

Our home was called The PLACE of CONSOLATION, as mother had and demonstrated real love to everyone. Her work gave her personal contact with ministers and their wives.

There was something about the suffering of ministers and their families that followed me from early childhood. It created a horrible picture in my mind. It was so dreadful I disdained the idea of being a minister's wife. I wanted to be a public speaker.

In addition, it was my desire to have a husband who could sing. The Lord granted my request. My husband is a gifted singer. He studied three years under Madame Robinson at the Trenton Conservatory of Music, and achieved great success.

This worked very well with my profession; as I did not want him to preach. He specialized in catering in schools and hotels. Three of his brothers also have musical careers.

The Lord blessed us to save money. Everything was pleasant. We were young, full of ambition, and had a desire to achieve success in life. We planned to buy a large home and a store.

One morning without the least provocation, we decided to give up housekeeping and visit cities, and be free from responsibilities. We put our furniture in storage, and boarded a train for New York City. This was Thursday afternoon. When we arrived in New York, we rented a room at six dollars per week, but we were discontented. On Sunday morning we boarded a train and went to Asbury Park, New Jersey. As it was a hot day, the city was crowded with weekend guests.

Seemingly all of the hotels and rooming houses were occupied. After walking for three hours, we found a room for which we paid the lady six dollars. I was so happy I prayed out on the porch.

We had drawn all of our money out of the bank; knowing we were worn and fatigued and very likely to fall into a deep sleep, I had to find a safe hiding place for the money. I had six hats in a box. Therefore I placed the money in one of the linings, pressed them together and went to bed.

About twenty minutes afterward someone screamed, "The house is burning down". I leaped out of bed, took my hatbox with the money, and ran as fast as I could. When the fire was extinguished we returned to our room, but I did not have any desire to sleep.

The next morning we arose discontented and planned to go far away, but my brother-in-law came, and we decided to go to Bayhead, New Jersey. We left that afternoon. They worked in a hotel while I vacationed on the Beach. This was a beautiful place. I had a real prayer meeting by the seaside. One afternoon while I was on the beach crocheting, a lady was attracted to me. She was looking for someone to be a companion to her and her daughter.

She offered me sixty dollars per month, and gave me permission to have my husband stay in the home with me. I accepted her offer. This was grand; I could pray, read my Bible, and save my money. I worked six weeks, and became dissatisfied. I went out to the hotel to tell my husband that I was discontented. I met him on the boardwalk enroute to tell me the same news. We adjusted matters where we worked, and boarded a train that afternoon for Philadelphia, Pennsylvania.

When we arrived in the city we went to the home of a sweet mother in Israel. Her home was known as the "Christians" Rest. She was an excellent cook and an immaculate housekeeper. The greetings and welcome she bestowed upon us were very gracious. She sent us to bed as happy as could be. My husband and I prayed together and retired. I adjusted myself to rest until the next morning. I had just fallen asleep when something like an electric shock went through me. I felt like someone was sticking pins in my body. I called my husband. He switched on the light, and there were ants, large red bugs, black bugs, white and gray bugs, and something that resembled a bug and worm made together. We leaped out of the bed and destroyed as many as we could, but they reinforced themselves. They were coming so fast, we were helpless. The surrounded us everywhere. I was so tired I spread a sheet on the floor, thinking I would be able to rest; but not so, they bit me through the sheet. They came through the cracks in the floor, the walls, and they were running on all the furniture. I put on my bedroom slippers and behold, they were in them. I never witnessed a time like this! My husband carried a quilt our on the roof, but they attacked him so badly our there they drove him back into the room. We dared not sleep, that army had surrounded our chairs, the only way we got any peace was to sit in a chair and draw our feet up; even then they dropped from the ceiling upon us.

Being afraid, I cried. When I asked my husband what caused this, his reply was, "God's war is on." I was embarrassed to meet the mother of the home the next morning. She was very sweet; she came to our room to have family prayer. When she observed what had happened she looked steadfastly into my husband's eyes. She pointed her finger and told him if he did not preach the Gospel, God would kill both of us. She asked him did he know the Lord was after him. He did not reply. She turned and asked me; "What are you trying to do, hold up the program of God?" I told her I did not want to hinder the Lord;

neither did I want my husband to preach. She told me he was born to preach, and the time had come for him to surrender. I was discouraged and disgusted; we packed our baggage and left at once.

We rented a room on Mt. Vernon Street at six dollars per week. This was an ideal opportunity for me to adjust myself to light housekeeping. The owner of the house was a businessman and had to be away most of the time. I called my husband in question and I cross-examined him concerning what he knew about being called to preach, but he would neither confirm nor deny.

A few days after we started a new life, the roaches made war with us again. They were in our food, in the bed and they ran over our faces; when we drew water from the spigot it looked like someone had put baby honeybees in it. If we bought anything from the store by the time we reached home it was filled with roaches. The man of the house was so amazed he questioned us. He asked my husband did he know he was Jonah. He told him the mark of the Lord was stamped upon him to preach the gospel, but he had rebelled and the Lord had permitted these plagues to contaminate him.

This did not suit me. We conversed together and decided it was better for him to return to his occupation in Jersey. I was confident this would relieve him from the information he had received from the sister and brother concerning preaching the gospel. The next day he rented a room for me with a dear Christian lady. He boarded a train for New Jersey but God's time had come. When he was half way between Philadelphia and Trenton, the Lord called him by name and asked him, "What are you going to do about preaching My Word?"

He knew it was the Lord speaking, but he did not answer. The train seemed as if it would wreck. The disturbances were so great; the engineer stopped the train and investigated the tracks. They started out again. The Lord told him so say, "Yes" that day or he would die. Conditions were very serious; and heaven's pressure was upon him. He said, "Yes, from this day on, I will preach."

The Lord accepted his acknowledgement. When he arrived in Trenton Railroad Station, he penned me a letter and asked me to forgive him for not telling me, but he was born to preach. He had been called since he was five and a half years old. He preached when he was a boy;

he said sometimes the desire burnt in his heart so strongly that he drove sticks in the ground on the outskirts of his father's farm and preached to them. He acknowledged he knew it was a great responsibility for me, but he had accepted it at any cost. When I received that special delivery letter I collapsed. It made me seriously ill. The people were afraid so they called a physician and he administered a needle, but it did not revive me. They read the letter and found the task was too great for me. They sent for my mother to rush to my bedside at once. When she arrived, she urged me to let God plan my life.

Well, I had to adjust myself and prepare for a new life. Three weeks later my husband visited me. His countenance had changed; his conversation was different. There was a deep, humble expression upon him. The fear of the Lord filled my heart. I decided not to rebel any longer; but to seek the Lord, and let Him make me what I did not want to be.

The time came when he was invited to preach his trial sermon. I took it in shorthand. His text was, "What Shall Separate Me from the Love of God?" He repeated this two hundred and fifty times. I had to enjoy it for there was no way out; I had to be wise; therefore, I encouraged him. I purchased the very best literature and books. I never invited him to read them, but I put them where they would attract his attention; then I prayed that the Lord would encourage his interest and He did. Thank God, He prepared him for this day. He is so far from where he started, my soul, my heart and all that is within me give glory unto our Maker.

His brother, Elder J.P. Dabney, was called to the ministry the same day. There is something about these two brothers to be admired. They were converted the same day, baptized on the same day and were ordained together. Both have the same taste in almost everything. They studied music together and achieved equal success; although they are not twins. I sought the Lord daily for wisdom, knowledge and understanding to be granted unto these two men. We were very young. The pitfalls of zeal without knowledge beckoned to us; but the Lord's hand guided us, taught us not to clamor for offices, neither to desire high places. We humbled ourselves and the Lord made a way. Many opportunities presented themselves to run to and from, but we refused and made our home our choice.

I discouraged the idea of early pasturing. This obligation at times is dangerous to a young minister. They accepted my counsel; therefore they never gave any leader a heavy heart. They waited to be examples and not problems. When I behold, and consider how God blessed Elder Dabney; I recalled that there is a family tree responsible for his ministerial character. He represents the fifth generation of ministers in his family. God blessed both of us to be reared in Christian homes, where the family altar was the center of attraction.

The Holy Bible was taught, obeyed and lived. We knew God when we were young. The Name of Jesus was hallowed both day and night. We deeply appreciate the Biblical training we received in our homes.

It prepared us to assume the responsibility of leadership in this age, which is far different because of lack of the family altar and fireside training. The children today eat and grow, most of them, without the knowledge of God their Maker, who gave them food and life.

It has been said, "good followers make good leaders." Be that as it may, I am confident of this fact, if a child follows the Lord's guidance, he or she will be recognized in this world and the world to come. I am enthused beyond expression when I think, God made everything good for His children to enjoy while they live. There is no more standing upon the stormy backs of muddy Jordan casting a wishful eye; but the children of the King are privileged to view, enjoy and possess whatever their Father presents to them.

When I worked in churches in New Jersey with my husband under Pastors and women Supervisors, I had a great desire to go to that place where the Christian women went in the ancient days.

They prayed and found God's favor and divine righteousness. He made Himself known unto them. I grew tired of everything I knew; there was something greater for me than gossiping and tale-bearing, or making myself a busy-body in other individuals' matters. Many times when the women assembled together I went off by myself; because I was very hungry for the Lord. I made my prayer altar under the bed, there I buried my face in my hands and wept, begging the Lord to let me talk with Him face to face.

Sometimes when I was praying, the people would ascend the fire escape and peep in my window to see what I was doing. They found me under my bed praying and weeping as though my heart would break. Pastor Thomas and his wife were precious people in the Gospel. They understood the way the Lord was leading me. They encouraged me to press forward as the Lord would come unto me while I was young. They told me He would reveal some of those gracious things He had reserved for His children, who walked uprightly. When I found out it was right to pay tithes, I made it the business of life. Everything the Lord blessed me with, whether I labored it or whether it was just a gift, I tithed.

"The Lord is merciful and just; He hideth the future behind the shadow of His hand, until the hand of His divine clock strikes the moment."

CHAPTER II

The Dark Days

In the year Nineteen Hundred and Twenty-five, the Lord led Bishop Mason to send Elder O.T. Jones from Little Rock Arkansas, to pastor the church in West Philadelphia, Pennsylvania, which was a large Mission over a garage.

My husband, his brother and I, were members of a church at Trenton, New Jersey. We were serving faithfully under Overseer Bryant and his co-worker, Mrs. Lula M. Cox. Elder Jones visited the New Jersey Conference and found us working faithfully, minding our own business, praying and assisting in whatever was necessary for the uplift of the Kingdom of God.

He was attracted and requested our New Jersey leaders to permit us to work with him in Philadelphia; since we were residents of that city. This favor was granted to him. He permitted my husband and his brother to assist him in his church work; he told me my work was to pray and write for the church.

We were very thankful, and served wholeheartedly. We had many tests, for the Mission over the garage was condemned. We had nowhere to go. We rented a lot and set up a large tent. God wonderfully blessed in the services, and through much fasting and prayer, many were saved and healed. The pastor was a man of much prayer; therefore he instilled the principles in us. His dear wife, Mother Cora Green, Mrs. L. Hasty and Mrs. H. Gottie were great helpers in building the work. Winter came and we had to find somewhere to go.

There was only one building available-an old dilapidated garage. When the owners found out the pastor and congregation were praying people, they charged us one hundred dollars per month. Many times, when we were on our knees praying in that place, the boiler would overflow and we would find ourselves in a puddle of water. That was a very, very cold winter. We had no comfort; but it did not discourage us from holding on to God.

When Spring came, we returned to the tent. The Lord blessed in such a wonderful way the devil sought to molest us. He put it into some individuals' hearts to destroy the tent by fire.

The pastor was in Norfolk, Virginia. When he returned and found my husband and his brother holding the people together, conducting services on the platform, with no shelter over them, tears coursed down his cheeks. We found a real friend and a brother in the pastor of St. Matthews A.M.E. Church, across the street from where he conducted tent services. He invited us into his church and shared a part of his church worship time with us.

Soon we found another tent. We prayed for God to give us a church nearby; our request was granted. One day while we were praying, a business man, who owned a store and dwelling house on fifty-seventh and Vine Streets, contacted our pastor and offered him the buildings for a church. The prayer service impressed him, therefore he was anxious to see us progress. He was a contractor and builder. We prayed, and God sent the money, and we built a beautiful church. I told the Lord I was not going out to do mission work anymore. I selected a seat on the front pew and made myself comfortable to work and complete my prayer ministry there.

But our ways are not God's ways. One Sunday morning, the pastor met my husband and told him it was time for us to get out and dig out a church for ourselves, before we grew too old. When he told me what the pastor said, it almost broke my heart.

II

I was tired and disappointed. I really did not see how I would be able to carry on and suffer any more in mission digging. The pastor offered my husband a church in Steelton, Pennsylvania and he made other offers. He also granted him the privilege of starting a church in North Philadelphia. I shall never forget how I begged him not to accept a church which had been pastured by inexperienced leaders. If we do not profit by the mistakes of others, we are making very little in life. I prayed and prevailed with him to accept North Philadelphia, which was a new field, knowing full well that we were capable with God's help and our prayer life, to do as much in this field as we had done in West Philadelphia. We left a well equipped church with a large membership and we never encouraged a single member to follow us.

Elder J.P. Dabney, my brother-in-law, went with us to North Philadelphia. He held on to God with us and worked faithfully until the pastor called him back to assume the responsibility as his assistant pastor. He was with us when we rented the building on Twenty-first and Sharswood Streets for twenty-eight dollars per month; seating capacity of forty. There were no windows, no ventilation, just a small transom over the door. This place was located in a very wicked neighborhood. There were three bootleggers in the building, one on the second floor, one on the third floor and one in the rear. The streets were lined with old men who played dominoes and checkers all day long. Their language was too profane for any human being to hear. This went on day and night.

We moved into this building Sunday afternoon, April sixth, Nineteen hundred and twenty-nine. Our pastor loaned us eighteen broken chairs and an old dilapidated pulpit stand which had been partly destroyed in the tent fire. He told us if the Lord gave us one soul in nine years, to count it as a blessing, and an encouragement from our heavenly Father. He told us not to come back; if we had been divinely called, our gift would make room for us, regardless of how much suffering we had to go through.

One afternoon I went to North Philadelphia to pray. The Lord called my attention to the situation in the neighborhood. I asked Him would He give us the victory, and break through the bonds, so that the gainsayers would have nothing to say; if I went under a covenant and vow with Him in prayer. He did not ask me to make the covenant; nor did He answer me speedily, but He said He would break through and bless; if I wanted to make the sacrifice. I asked Him where did He want me to meet Him to make my vow.

He told me to meet Him the next morning at the Schuylkill River at seven-thirty o'clock. The river is known to Philadelphians as

Riverside Drive. I gave Him my promise that I would be there. I went home and found my husband resting. I asked him if he would carry me to Riverside Drive the next morning. He was amazed; he arose excited, and inquired why I wanted to be there at seven-thirty. I told him it was very necessary. He went back to bed, but I pulled his feet. I talked with him until his sleep disappeared. After he discovered that I meant to go there, he consented to go with me.

I was so afraid I would miss the appointment with the Lord, I sat up all night and crocheted. I dared not put my trust or confidence in an alarm clock. I left home in plenty of time to meet the Lord. When we came to the place, where a tree bent over the road, the Lord said: "This is the Place." I told my husband not to follow me; I would return shortly. I descended the hill, and ran to the bank of the river. Just before me were two large stones, at the edge of the water, there was a little stone.

I had no prepared speech or essay; I did not write an address; I was not in a position to give a lecture. Believe me, when I tell you, I did not know what to expect. As I stood between the two large stones, the presence of God overshadowed me, and I acknowledged.

I lifted my eyes heavenward and said, "Lord, if you will bless my husband in the place You sent him to establish Your name, if You will break the bonds and destroy the middle wall or partition; if You will give him a church and congregation-a credit unto Your people and all Christendom, I will walk with You for three years in prayer; both day and night. I will meet You every morning at nine o'clock sharp; You will never have to wait for me; I will be there to greet You. I will stay there all day; I will devote all of my time unto You." I walked forward about five or six steps, and stood on the little stone which was at the edge of the water. I said unto Him, "Furthermore, if You will hearken unto the voice of my supplication and break-through in that wicked neighborhood, and bless my husband, I will fast seventy-two hours each week for two years. While I am going through the fast, I will not go home to sleep in my bed. I will stay at church; if I become sleepy I will rest on newspapers and carpet."

As soon as I had made this covenant unto the Lord the heavens opened on that river bank; and the glory of the Lord fell from heaven all around me. It fell in the water like large drops of hail and rain. I knew he had prepared me to enter into this Prayer Ministry Suffering. He let me know very definitely that it had to be real, wholehearted prayer business to keep covenant.

I am unable to tell you how I felt, or to describe what it means to enter into such a covenant with the Lord.

Taking a memorandum book from my handbag; I tore out three pieces of paper and wrote the covenant.

I ascended the hill and found Elder Dabney waiting with his eyes open to the utmost extent. I do not know what he thought about introducing me into this new field, but I am confident he was alarmed.

I told him the covenant I had made. I asked him if he would permit me the privilege and opportunity to fulfill this obligation; but he flatly refused. He tried to make me go home. I told him I would never return home again until he agreed to let me pray. I pleaded and finally I told him the Lord would kill me if I broke this covenant. He looked at me amazed. He told me it was not six months; it was not just a year; three years was too long for anybody to obligate herself to pray night and day, especially going to church daily at that early hour, and undergoing the suffering this would demand.

I made it very clear to him my life was doomed if he rejected. I wept and the Lord touched his heart; he gave me his consent. He asked when would I enter into this Prayer Life. "Tomorrow morning," I replied. My heart leaped for joy; this was the happiest moment I ever experienced to do something for God.

The next morning at nine o'clock I met the Lord on time. I became so accustomed to meeting Him at that hour, I never had to look at my clock to find out the correct time; however I did.

At nine o'clock each morning the door know of the church would turn. I knew it was the Lord; therefore I greeted Him with a hearty, "Good morning, Jesus."

His glory filled the room all day long. He was my guest. I would sit down and pray; I kneeled until I wore all the skin off of my knees on those hard floors. They were so sensitive, many times I was in great pain; however I had to use them without murmuring or complaining. At times I was so worn in my body. I placed three chairs together and stretched out on them. At times I crocheted and prayed. I never permitted anything to interfere with my conversation with God. I suffered. The flesh on my bones was numb; I fasted, not eating or drinking natural food; but I had a direct supply from heaven. The days were dark, and I did not see my way; but of one thing I was confident, the Lord guided my footsteps; I enjoyed His company and He enjoyed mine.

Soon that mission was too small to accommodate the people; my husband requested me to pray for another place nearby. I prayed; and a business man who had been in business for twenty-five years decided to sell out, and rent the building to us. This building was located on the opposite side of the street. Just a stone's cast from where the first building was located. By this time, I realized that the Lord was showing me some of His glory, while He had me hid away in His prayer cleft. The new landlord charged us ninety dollars per month. I did not know where one penny was coming from; but we accepted it by faith. I did not pray and leave my home uncared for. I got up early each morning and performed my home duties. The seventy-two hours I fasted and remained in church, my husband and little son looked after my obligations to keep me from worrying. The people did not understand why I should devote so much of my time to church.

These were not sinners, but they professed the same love of God I had. They did not want me to pray. Many times they warned my husband of the danger and embarrassment I would cause him, our child and the church, if he did not stop me from praying. The declared that I was mentally deranged and would soon be a case for the psychopathic ward.

Not only did they try to discourage him, but many times they would come to church and pull and shake me, trying to make me leave the prayer altar. I recognized their voices. I knew the devil sent them there. I never opened my eyes. I was on the prayer elevator going up! I just elbowed my way. When the devil could not defeat me by tormenting me with visitors, he put out a diabolical propaganda that I was n "old witch; a magic book reader" and a "mastermind woman." This falsehood took the wings of the morning and it flew wherever the devil sent it. So much was said, the people came to see what type of individual I was.

When they came and found my tear-stained face and much sacrificed life, wholly surrendered, praying for the Lord to manifest His glory in that place, they repented with tears for even permitting the devil to sow such evil seed in their minds. They found the old path Daniel, the Hebrew boys, and the Apostle Paul traveled. The devil did not permit this to be gossip to me; but he made the people bold enough to ask me to let them read my "magic book." The Lord was so sweet in my soul I never sought any information from my adversaries, nor would the Lord let it grieve me. He amused me with the Scriptures, and He supported me with His arms.

CHAPTER III

Angels Guard The Highway

At eight o'clock one morning, I went to church to read my bible before my prayer hour. When I opened the door, there was a piece of paper with three hearts drawn in red and black ink, and a dagger. On it was printed these words in bold-faced type: "Get out of this neighborhood at once. We do not want your prayer meetings."

This was the time I had to be a wise woman; I did not tell Elder Dabney. I knew he would suggest moving, but this was not the best thing; therefore I pondered these words in my heart and continued praying. About five months later, I found another paper under the door addressed to me. The three hearts were larger, a dagger pierced each one, and the blood streamed freely. The warning stated, "We have warned you to get out of this neighborhood with your prayer meetings; you are too simple and crazy about that God of yours to pay attention. This comes to let you know if you get off the trolley car Thursday morning you will never pray again. You had better pay attention to this as we are a group who hates your prayer meetings."

I showed the paper to a dear woman of God who was faithful to me. She begged me not to go by trolley, but to call a cab. I told her I would not pay any attention to any of the devil's demands. I begged her not to tell my husband. I know God was able to protect my life, as I had committed no crime, neither had I interfered with any individual's business. I did not pray loud in the building; I knew I lived godly.

Thursday morning, my cup was running over. I talked with God. I related unto Him the story of my covenant. I reminded Him of the words He had spoken to me at the river bank. "It must be business continually." He did not tell me what to do. When I got off the trolley car, I saw two men standing on opposite corners. They watched the trolley as if they were looking for someone, but they did not molest me.

One of them started towards me, my heart was praying so loud it seemed as if it went to the bottom of my feet, and they joined in prayer with me. I did not run. I called on the Name of Jesus. I requested Him to let the blood cover me completely. I know He answered my prayers immediately, for the man stopped following me. I missed his footsteps. I knew that the Spirit of the Lord had prevailed for me and the angel of the Lord guarded the highway.

I did not do like Lot's wife, I did not look back. Down in my soul I heard a multitude singing; "Be not dismayed, whatever besides, God will take care of you." That was one morning my tears fell on the street. The front of my dress was soaking wet, I cried until I reached the church door. No one would ever imagine the sermons the devil preached to me from the trolley to the church.

I felt like a deserted individual who had been given to the wild beasts to be destroyed without a cause. I never permitted myself to accuse my dear kind Father, for after all, I had made the covenant with Him.

I was aware of His divine leading; it was my choice.

When I opened the church door and went in, I was impressed to lock it. I fell on my face and wept until tears were on the floor as if someone had poured water.

I thanked Him for protecting my life; I felt His arms embracing me, as a child would feel the arms of her father. The fragrance from Him was so sweet, I feasted. Although I had experienced this great ordeal, I realized the Lord had taught me a wonderful lesson as to what it means to suffer for Christ.

Our son was very obedient; my husband was kind, sympathetic and understanding. I was not disagreeable at home; I served wholeheartedly. A good housewife with Christian experience and wisdom will make a good church mother. The Lord saved our little son when he was nine and a half years old. Our baby passed three weeks before we went to North Philadelphia to open the Mission. Our son had to make great sacrifices also. I taught him the responsibilities of helping to dig out the church. He knows something about personage experience; but he was delighted.

Our first offering raised for the church was thirty-five cents. I thought this was wonderful and it was; the Lord sent it. I was not able to buy expensive clothes. We had our home obligations and we had to look after the church in every detail; naturally I had to use wisdom.

I wanted to be presentable. I purchased gingham at fifteen cents per yard and made plain, pleated dresses. The Lord sent dear Brother and Mother Bell and her sister, Miss Decator. Brother Bell is one of the pioneers of this work; Mother Bell and her sister cared for my laundry; this was a blessing from God.

This is the prayer I prayed each morning before I left home, while I was under the covenant.

> Dear God, thank you for the morning light
> This day I have lived to see.
> Guide my speech, order my feet aright
> As I leave this place, to meet Thee.
> I praise you for your training school,
> The teaching you do impart,
> Make me one of your praying tools:
> Abide within my heart.
> As I leave this home you gave;
> Dear God, protect it for me.
> Let the blood of Jesus save.
> My prayers ascend to Thee.
> If it pleases you to call me home
> Before my covenant ends today,
> Let me rest in Thine arms;
> Accept this prayer I pray.
> Bless all the Leaders of the land;
> Bless everybody everywhere.
> The time has come; I must be on my way.
> Look for me I shall meet you there.

When we started the work, all types and classes of people came. This usually occurs whenever a new mission door opens. Sometimes those who come are honest hearted people, and their help proves beneficial.

Wherever the children of God assemble to worship, the devil always sends his angels to see what they can do to prevent the minister from raising the Christian banner.

Some individuals think the minister and workers should be able to discern the devil in everybody who comes to church and put him out. But not all of the hypocrites and false pretenders are in the streets. Very often I find them seated on the front pews in the church building. I will admit when they see the glory manifested in Zion they are surprised; but they are there. Experience teaches the gospel workers the ways of wisdom in church building.

It would be a wonderful thing if everybody who joined the church joined it for the express purpose of doing those things which please Jesus; but when an individual hears the Word and then becomes careless and loses the vision of the Cross and Calvary; when he fails to recognize the blood of Jesus; when he loses his Christian behavior and spiritual etiquette for God's house, beware! The fallen state of that soul will lead downward to death and destruction.

One night a minister and his wife joined our mission. He was a humble man of prayer; he paid his tithes properly. She was an excellent singer; she said the Lord told her to bring her husband there to help build his ministerial career. In every new field of Christian work, the pastor appreciates workers who give themselves wholly to God. But if they fail to follow Christ they will cause much trouble and end up in a wreck. As soon as this woman met me, she objected to my prayer life and she tried to turn the people against prayer and consecration. The devil put it in her heart to sow seeds of discord among the young converts. As soon as the Lord saved a soul she made it her business to visit his or her home early in the morning; and she spent much of her time there with them. When she left, they were spiritually dead; they did not have any desire to return to pray. She told them all of the male members had to give their family earnings to me, and all of the women were forced to give all of their income to Elder Dabney. You understand what publicity of this type would do in a new, uncultivated field. The husbands and wives of these young converts were sinners. They did not profess Christ nor were they interested in any religious worship.

One evening this minister collapsed in the church. He had been ill. Breath left his body. He was getting cold and stiff. His wife looked upon his body and sent for the doctor in order that she might be able to call for the undertaker. The Spirit of the Lord came upon my husband and his brother. They prayed for half an hour, and the Lord restored him to life again. This was the first time this woman had witnessed God's divine power as it was manifested that night-she was amazed. Naturally, she tried to be good for a while, but the devil tempted her, and she continued working mischief among the people of God. One day while her husband was working in a large department store here in Philadelphia, he met with a serious accident. He was using a hose which had poison acid in it. The top came off, and his eyes were burned. He was a terrible sight. They rushed him to the hospital and to a specialist; they said the acid had burned the ball of his eyes completely out. They carried him home. He begged to be led to church and while he sat in the prayer meeting, the spirit of the Lord came upon my husband and his brother. As they prayed for God to manifest Himself that night, this man's eyes came open! They were perfect. When he went back to the physician he was greatly amazed. This stirred the hearts of the people; many believed and were saved.

When we moved into the second building across the street, it seemed a ripe time for the ingathering of souls. By this time many of our members had learned how to contact God in prayer; they were ready for the battle. The Lord sent shower after shower of blessings upon us, and the devil sent this woman from place to place warning the people not to come there. Jealousy filled her heart, and she eyed me continually. God was breaking the bonds and my soul was enjoying the benefits. She grew vile and wicked. She told a falsehood, and went to the Municipal Court and swore out a warrant for my arrest. She gave them the church address. Two men came to deliver the warrant. They came into the church, but the presence of God was so great they did not advance forward to where I was. They sat in the rear of the building and penned a note asking me if I would stop praying long enough to answer a few questions. One of our members gave me the note. I had been weeping before the Lord. I did not try to dry my tears before going to them. From the way they acted, I am sure they realized that God was with me. They were very kind, but so fearful their hands trembled. They read the charge that they had against me; it seemed as if the Christ in my soul stood up and spoke for Himself. They did not rebut; they understood immediately why this accusation had been made. They shook hands with me, and told me not to worry; but pray for them.

They were very anxious for me to prosecute her, but I told them I had an attorney in heaven looking after my case. I was waiting for Him to call me to court. When prayer defeated her in this wise, murder filled her heart. She purchased a new butcher knife, and had it sharpened, she sent me word to pack my belongings, close the mission doors and leave North Philadelphia at once.

She was tired of my foolish prayer meetings all day and all night. The meetings did not disturb her peace, she did not live nearby; besides in all the prayer services I conducted, I never made unnecessary noise and I trained our members to wait on the Lord in quietness. One afternoon she showed the butcher knife to a group of women. She told them she was going to help me and my covenant in prayer. The rebuked her, and warned her of the danger which was ahead for interfering with such a consecrated work as ours was; but she refused to give heed to counsel. One afternoon while I was praying in church, she related her threats to a dear old, precious mother who visited her and advised her to give up these thoughts and ideas which could only mean trouble to her and all concerned.

She was angry. She went to her sink to get some water. The hand of God's wrath struck her. She fell to the floor; blood ran from her ears, nose and mouth. She struggled in great pain. He knew she had gone far enough; it was at this hour He demanded an answer from her why she permitted Satan to tempt her to sin against the Holy Spirit and His people. They sent for her husband; he carried her to the hospital. All the way there she called for me. They could hardly put her into the hospital bed. She told the doctors and the nurse she had treated me wrongfully. She begged them to give her something to keep her from dying until I arrived. She said everything before her was dark, that she had to get things straight with me. Otherwise her soul would be lost. When the news came to me, I was praying in church at my prayer altar.

Angels Guard The Highway

I rushed as fast as I could to the hospital, but when I entered the nurse said, "You are too late; she left fifteen minutes ago". It is very unwise to permit the devil to make you a terror unto good works. It is unwise to give yourself over to jealousy. Workers and ministers are more than dumb creatures and cowards; they have to suffer much; but when God gets ready to avenge, it will be serious time.

Each one should remember there is no mercy seat in the grave. There is no altar where one can go to repent. Whenever we fail to adjust our mistakes before the end, it must be settled on that final day at the bar of justice. Sometimes the devil makes people think that because no one is around to tell the news, they are privileged to abuse and mistreat their fellow workers and friends; but there is a recording machine in God's studio. Everything we say and do is recorded. After a while the transcription will be played, and there will be no place to make excuses.

In this world intellectuality, shrewdness and outward appearance often give an individual the ability to lead a multitude regardless of how they live, but one should never go too high not to remember that there is a heaven; that there is a throne of judgment, and all wise, supreme and just God. When the final day comes, if it pleases Him to review our lives by transcription; or read it from the records, we shall hear and give an accurate account of our stewardship.

I never mention this woman's name in public, nor did I permit envy to enter my heart or mind. She was used by Satan to hinder my spiritual success; but I had great love in my heart for her. The accusations did not hinder the Lord from elevating my life nor promoting spiritual growth. I am confident if her life had been spared until I arrived at her bedside in the hospital. I would have prayed for the Lord to forgive her sins and save her soul.

CHAPTER IV

A Vision Of The Future

After this building was overcrowded, Elder Dabney said, he did not want to rent another building, he wanted to buy a place where he would be able to call it, "The Lord's Property." He requested me to ask my kind Savior to send the money. I sought Him diligently and in three months time, He sent us fifteen hundred dollars.

We purchased a church just around the corner. This building had been used for the Masonic Temple; also for a furniture warehouse. When we entered with our little congregation, it seemed as if we had just started. It had a balcony on both sides and a large pipe less heater in the basement. The street was large and congested; it was not properly ventilated.

Elder Dabney spent many nights with me there in prayer, but most of the time he went home to be with our son. When winter came, I suffered more than I shall ever be able to tell. We were unable to buy fuel, enough to heat the building for the evening services and make it comfortable for those who prayed with me when we fasted seventy-two hours therefore, we wrapped ourselves in blankets and quilts to keep warm. Sometimes I was so cold my whole body was numb; but those faithful praying church mothers and daughters of mine drew near to me. Some lad their heads in my lap, some put their arms around my shoulders and others lay down on either side of me. There were so many of them around me I could not move, but their warm bodies warmed me.

Sometimes they went to sleep in that position, I could hardly breathe, they were so heavy, but I did not disturb them. They worked each day and had made the sacrifice to help me. Many times I wept over them and nobody knows what comfort they gave me. One of the young women whom I call "Sparrow" came in praying. She prayed so sincerely for the Lord to protect my health, it was like being around a live wire. The spirit of prayer broke out and those children prayed for me and wept before the Lord until all of my tired feelings disappeared.

It was not a loud, annoying sound, but each one prayed with one accord. Sparrow came over where I was kneeling and asked me, "What did God think about a group of children who loved Him well enough to stay in a place like that day and night without eating or drinking?"

I told her it was impossible for me to explain to her what was in the dear mind of God our Father but, I was confident, a few steps ahead she would find the answer if she kept climbing the midnight mountain. Many of those women who prayed with me all night and all day were not members of our particular church, but they were Christians, honest hearted workers and representatives of God from various churches.

God taught me very definitely that it as wrong and against His divine order to make a difference between His children. A child of God, a Christian, a Saint and a soldier of the cross are all the same. They must live together here and it is their obligation and duty to follow peace and love without dissimulation. When the pastors found out I was honest in my heart and not a church wrecker, many of them consented for their members to pray with me. They treated me royally; they made it just as pleasant for me as the members of our church. Today, when they hear how God has blessed my work in the ministry of prayer and suffering, they are living witnesses because they went through the conflict with me.

When we consider what God has done, we must say it was in His divine plan. To be misunderstood, you will be misrepresented. The thing that makes it so distressing is, when an individual does not understand another and then closes the door of opportunity to become acquainted.

It was never my desire, nor shall it ever be, to pull down, to molest or to undermine any body. I am very careful how I speak concerning those who represent the same Christ I represent. I never tolerate anyone's teaching that one Christian in better than another. In our abilities, in talent, in wealth we find one more blessed than the other, but in this Christian warfare the individual who to the glory of God. They can extend greetings to the poor, share a part of their possessions with the unfortunate, live in peace with all men and do those things which please the Lord just as well as that individual who has all knowledge and wisdom. The sooner we learn this lesson, the sooner our advancement in consecration and righteousness will become a beacon light for this lost, dying, distressed, blind world.

If we are saved from sin, nothing can be greater. If we had been bought with a price by the blood of Jesus, then we are children of the King.

Nothing will ever be able to pull us down or separate us from the divine fellowship the Lord gives us here. I repeat, it does not make any difference what we know, what we possess, where we have gone or where we are, if we are Christians, there is no difference. If divisions arise, it is because the motive is wrong and the plan is carnal. Nobody can pray through into the glory of God as long as they feel up today and down tomorrow.

This life is like an ocean. Sometimes wisdom rolls up the curtain of the day, ties back the draperies of the hour, raises the window of joy; throughout our entire being we feel the cool breeze of peace and contentment penetrating, yeah even the marrow in our bones seems to respond to its touch. Life is made up this way. Suddenly, while we behold the element, the cloud heads can be seen from afar, floating, making themselves into a carpet or a canvas. Down in our souls, the hunger and thirst tells us that it's moving on towards God's noon hour when we need to put aside every thing and eat His Word. "Eat much of it", "eat until we are full and then store away the fragments". We know it is the noon hour, we can hear the songs of praises singing in the music room of our souls.

Suddenly we hear something dashing upon this old ship of life. When we look out, the "sun of all that joy and singing" has disappeared.

Troubles, trials and tribulations come skipping down "life's briny deep" and those clouds which formed a beautiful picture of a Biblical scene a few moments hence, are now angry and black, almost as night. They are rolling to and fro; from somewhere behind God's testing rock, the wind blows. It does not make any difference how many degrees we have obtained or in what position or class we rank.

When the sea becomes troubled, the ship pays no regard unto anyone. It just rocks from side to side. If the children are asleep, if the sick are in pain, if the family is languishing, if the aged are convalescing in their reclining chairs, if death summons has entered, it makes no difference; just stay on board. Remember this is a sailor's life.

Since it is true the "Gospel Ship" is on life's sea of time, sometimes conditions make it impossible to go forward, but we dare not go backward against the contrary winds. This is where we find the need of the "anxious altar and the mercy sea" to be in our hearts. We can converse with God when we cannot utter a word, prayer becomes more realistic than just a desire of the heart, uttered or unexpressed. It gives you a vision of the future. It becomes a reality or in other words, it is a stream, a method or an instrument that opens the way for the children of God to enter into "His guest chamber." Thank God for that prayer that brings Christ and His children into personal contact. It locks the mouths of those "hungry sea monsters" who ride the waves of time seeking food.

It goes further than that, it overpowers the minds of high and great men, it goes beyond palaces and leads a contrite, pure hearted individual into the courts of glory.

Once you enter the "Holy of Holies" there will be no danger of leaving without personal contact with the Father of the universe and His Son who gave His life, His blood and endured all things for us. I admit there are times on this ocean when we do not always experience Him by feelings, but we know He is on the ship. He entered life's sea boat when we left Egypt's shores of sin. An individual who walks with God, is never absolutely cold spiritually, although sometimes there is no manifestation or outward demonstration, but in the heart the prayer fire burns. It is not a homemade prayer. It is not a selfish prayer. No one can make time and ride the seas of doubt and overcome the sea horses and sea whales unless they are acquainted with that source of prayer that reaches everybody everywhere.

An individual must know how to defeat the devil and claim the victory. Satan will never permit our daily record to receive "passing mark" if he is permitted to carry out his program. We must be wise when it comes to this Christian warfare. We do not have to study a course on how to love each other.

We love because Jesus lives in our hearts. We have a vision of that great "love feast" we shall have when the table of the Lord is spread and the invitation has been given to "Come and dine" in that great day when the Lord shall come for His children. After the Lord opened unto us a prayer school in North Philadelphia, it was my Christian duty to treat all of His students alike. If an individual had a pure heart and wanted to sacrifice time and sleep to pray with me, my heart and soul encouraged him to do so. The Lord saved hundreds of children.

I took them into my confidence and cared for them as my own. They learned how to agonize until they received help from beyond the hills. They loved the Word of God. It has been taught that children are too young to serve the Lord, but from my childhood the Lord followed me.

Chapter V

My Covenant Ends

One morning I arose early after I had completed my homes duties. I was impressed to go to church earlier than usual. I lived thirty-one blocks from the church and had to board two trolley cars.

The Lord was with me as never before. I felt victory in my soul; it was real joy, unspeakable. I was pure and clean in my heart, thanksgiving, praises and adoration ascended unto Him. The wheels of the trolley seemed to be praying with me, my cup ran over and I fought bravely to restrain the tears. The trolley car was so crowded. I did not want any demonstration. I did not realize it was the end of my covenant. When I unlocked the church door, the glory of the Lord met me and pulled me in, as usual I greeted Him with, "GOOD MORNING, JESUS!"

He said to me, "Go back home." His voice was not as it had been. I was amazed, but I did not demonstrate. I ran as fast as I could trying to make it to my prayer altar.

Midway the aisle, all my strength left me. I fell on my knees. His voice sounded again like an angry man, "GO BACK HOME!" I looked forward to the ceiling and inquired of Him what crime had I committed that offended Him. I was brokenhearted. It seemed to me as if I was in the deepest trouble and sorrow I had ever been in my life. His manner was not what I had expected. I thought as far back as I could go into the past. I could not find a thing to explain His displeasure at this hour, absolutely I had done all that I could and given all that I had. I wept bitterly. I wrung my hands with grief. I knew the end of all things was at hand for me. Suddenly my strength came, I leaped and ran forward trying to make it to my prayer altar before nine o'clock, but He uttered those words like thunder and many waters, "GO BACK HOME." By this time I was helpless. I fell near the altar, my handbag went one way and my Bible the other.

I felt like someone who had suffered a stroke. I screamed and cried as loud as I could. I asked Him what had separated our fellowship, what had disrupted our communion, what changed His attitude toward me. I told Him the people would molest me now, surely they would slander me as never before. I would never be able to show them what good I had derived from walking with Him. I asked Him to observe my record. If I had displeased Him, I was willing to make it right. I said, "Please tell me, dear God, what happened?" He said, in a calm voice, sweeter than anything I had ever heard, "*Your three years are up.*" You have prayed through into my glory. My strength came, it seemed as if the world lifted from my poor shoulders. I thought how wonderful it would be to rest in my home, in my bed again. I thought how sweet it would be to eat another square meal at my own table, I thought of the pleasure of being relieved from the hunger pains I had suffered while going through. Oh! Friends, I was hungry many times. I was so much in need of food, the devil told me to lick some of the dust from the cracks in the floor and swallow it, but I did not. I was so thirsty I felt like sucking the back of my hand to moisten my mouth which was dry and hot, but I did not.

When I realized that this was the end of my covenant, I just could not understand, I laughed for joy. I looked at the piece of paper I wrote at the river bank, there it was, three years ago I had said yes to God.

I staggered to my chair where I always prayed. I requested the Lord not to send me home, but grant me the privilege to stay in the building all day and make love to Him. By this time the building was full of His glory. I could feel His everlasting arms around me. He told me He did not want me to stay there, He wanted me to go home. Naturally I obeyed Him. When I got off the trolley on Fifty-sixth street, near where I live, there was a great change in my soul and in the world around me. The heavens, the tree tops, the house tops, everything was praising God in these words, seemingly the sunshine joined in the great refrain, "*You have prayed through into my glory.*"

The children had been dismissed from school for recess, they waved greetings to me, but I was too full to respond; therefore I ran as fast as I could trying to make it to my house.

"The heavens declare the glory of God; and the firmament sheweth His handiwork."-Psalm 19:1

When I opened my door, the Lord pushed me in the house. The door closed behind me; I became afraid, my bones began to tremble; I started up stairs, but His presence met me on the steps. It was under my feet, it was in the hall. I rushed into my room, I may as well have entered into the door of heaven. I told the Lord to please let me be satisfied with what He had given me. I wanted to go into the street. My son was in school; my husband had gone to eulogize the dead. I had no help. I told the Lord I had gotten myself into a terrible predicament by praying so long. This did not alter His affection or manifestation; the waves of glory were sweeping over me continually. I was like a helpless ship on a tempestuous ocean. The carpet on the floor was like glass; I tried to adjust myself by holding on to my bed; it was like ice and made my hands slip off. I staggered near the dresser and put out my hands to grasp it for protection, it moved out of my way. I staggered like a drunken woman.

The Lord commanded me to sit down. I could feel His arms around me like a dear father or a grand-father. He said unto me, My servant, you made a covenant with me three years ago. You vowed to keep it praying and fasting. You have kept your vow; you did not break it; this day I come to bless you, raise your hands and say 'Yes' unto your God.

I praised Him until the fear disappeared. Singing and music broke out in my soul. I sang about my furniture, my rug, the draperies and even the flowers that were in the dress I wore. My, I thought this was worth suffering for. I never experienced such a glorious afternoon in my life. This feast lasted until four o'clock that afternoon. The unction lifted. The Lord said unto me, "Go into your basement; I shall meet you there." I pleaded earnestly with Him not to send me to the basement, for I always disliked basements. For some reason I never cared for bungalows, they were always too near to the surface of the earth. I told Him I was ready to die, but I did not want to die in the basement, neither was it my desire to pass into the beyond before my husband returned home. I had saved a sum of money for my son's education (his father did not know this) therefore, I asked Him to let me live long enough to adjust these matters, then I would be ready to yield up the ghost.

The Lord shook me and commanded me again to meet Him in the basement. I went over to my desk to write the information and leave it where my husband would see its contents, but my hands were so heavy I could not lift the pen, they felt as if weights were on them.

I felt the hands of the Lord pushing me out of the door. I had a new pair of patent leather pumps, I had never worn. I put them on my feet and went to the basement as a convict would walk to the electric chair to be executed. I did not know where the Lord would meet me. When I came to the furnace, a light came out of the coal bin which overshadowed and blinded my natural vision.

A spigot turned on in the ceiling and the oil of the Lord ran upon me until I was encased about eight inches thick. It was like being placed in a closet. I was to that place I could not think, all human help had disappeared, my flesh and self never offered resistance-this was a glorious scene. Satan knew the Lord was preparing me for this prayer battle. He told me I would strangle to death. I had always especially feared death by strangulation or by fire. When he reminded me of this, I tried to raise my hands to my nose, but there was no response. I was absolutely helpless. I just said, "Amen" to God in my heart. I lifted my head heavenward and submitted to Him for His will to be done. When this ceased, the Lord appeared before me with a paper in his hand. He said, "You made the covenant, you vowed; you did not break it; this day *I have anointed you with the gift of soul saving, wherever you shall go and pray souls shall be delivered out of bondage. Both men, women, girls and boys. Thou shall not add unto my program. The day you add socials, styles and finance to help yourself, I will lift my anointing from you. While you pray, I will send finance to help my suffering pastors and the church. I will also take care of you.*

"*Thou shall see it, behold I tell you it shall come to pass, while you are praying, all nations shall come and pray with you. Do not be selfish, be wise, be faithful, be kind and diligent. If you obey, I will make thee a blessing unto the people.*"

With a few other instructions He passed off the scene. By this time, it seemed as if I had entered into "His Guest Chamber of splendor and delight." A band of music came out of the coal bin and I shouted until the heels came off of those new shoes. It was the sweetest music I have ever heard. It seemed as if I was shouting so high I had a platform in the air. A few minutes after five o'clock this anointing lifted. I ascended the steps with those heelless new shoes on my feet. When I entered the living room, my husband came in.

Then I remembered it was for him to be blessed for kingdom building, it was for his edification and the saving of souls that I had suffered.

I ran as fast as I could, with my arms outstretched to meet him, but I fell at his feet. I was unable to relate the story unto him. He was aquatinted with the responsibility I had endured. He knew what soul breaking heartrending pains I had suffered, trying to make life worthwhile for others. He picked me up and carried me upstairs to our bedroom. He knew it was too much for a human being to undergo, therefore he thought the end had come. He accused himself and wept over my still, cold, lifeless body.

He laid his hands upon me and asked the Lord to heal my body and restore life and strength; when he touched me I was so charged with the presence of the Lord, it knocked his hands away. He tried to help me the second time, but he experienced the same thing.

Then he decided, if I was dead, the glory of God was in it. Joy filled his soul. He praised the Lord and shouted. When I reacted he was very happy. I related to him the story, I called his attention to the piece of paper he had in his pocket recording the covenant I had made at the river bank. I told him, "as I live my three years expired today." He could not believe it, but when he saw the contents of the paper it verified my statement. We rejoiced together; he was interested and delighted to know I would be able to live a normal life again.

He had been so despondent after beholding the way in which I had suffered, just for the Gospel's sake and for his ministry to be a success. He said he had been to the mission more than a hundred times to make me go home and give the idea up, but each time the Lord encouraged him to let me go to the end of my journey.

I was new altogether, a soldier completely equipped to work in the army of the Lord, praying for everybody everywhere, "holding on for their deliverance and facing the issues of life as they would be presented unto me in this great prayer ministry." I thought, since I had experienced the presence of the Lord in such a wonderful way, I would not have to be bothered by Satan and his forces as I had been, but I am persuaded the more the Lord blesses an individual, the greater are the demands and suffering. I told my husband to permit me to dress and to carry me before "a theater, a ballroom or a saloon that night and let me pray." I had so much of the Lord's material in my heart and soul I wanted to see how it would be manifested. I thought of how wicked the people were and this would be an opportune time for prayer to be offered. He prevailed with me to be satisfied and go to church, and let the people know how much patience the Lord had given me to walk with Him. There was a time in that building that night. My husband permitted me to conduct a three weeks' revival; he went to Uniontown, Pennsylvania to visit an old friend, Elder Carr. I was very happy for him to leave me, for the first time and go far away. I wanted a test meeting or in other words, I wanted the Lord to show me how the prayers revival would be conducted.

CHAPTER VI

God's Approval And Manifestation

One afternoon I went to church, I placed six chairs before the altar, I knelt in prayer alone. High school girls passed by the building and heard me praying and groaning. They thought we were having an afternoon service and were impressed and came in. This had to be God's leading. I was there alone and I was groaning within myself very softly. Some of them left, but five decided I was so pitiful and sad they would pray with me. The Lord saved those five that afternoon, and demonstrated to me how He would work while I prayed for everybody everywhere.

After this, the devil continued to use unwise individuals to press the charge of witchcraft against me.

The attack was so humiliating, I almost decided to give up the life of prayer and live an isolated life away on a farm somewhere.

One day I visited a convention; the accusation I received was so disgraceful I almost collapsed, but I endured for the Gospel's sake. It hurt my husband's heart to see me mistreated for nothing so he sent me to Fairfield, Maryland for a rest.

I tried my best to be quiet, but Pastor Parker said the Lord had sent me there to pray. I told him I was almost afraid to conduct a prayer meeting; the people were so bitter against me for praying. He would not accept this, therefore I prayed in his church. The Lord saved seventeen souls. Fear came over me, I told the Pastor I would have to close the meeting at once. It rained hard that night, but God touched the hearts of the people, they gave me forty-two dollars as a love token and I prepared to go home. I was so excited, I forgot I had a telephone in my home, therefore I sent my husband a telegram to meet me at

30th Street Station. When he greeted me, he knew I was in distress. He knew the vacation did not refresh me, neither had I received any strength to carry on. I told him I did not know what happened, that I had prayed and the Lord had saved a goodly number of souls; I was very sorry it happened, but the Lord surprised me. He comforted me by saying, "God has blessed you, and no man shall be able to defeat you in your work."

The next day as we were sitting at that table, the telephone rang, it was the voice of Pastor Kelsey, of Washington, D.C. He was despondent because his tent service had been unsuccessful. He requested Elder Dabney to send me at once, but he refused, thinking I was too tired in my body. My heart seemed as if it was melting within me. I excused myself from the table, I ran upstairs as fast as I could. I fell on my knees and wept bitterly before the Lord.

My husband ran after me; he lifted me up and asked me if I really wanted to go. I told him, "Yes." My insurance was paid; I just felt like I wanted to die in Washington, D.C. He called Pastor Kelsey and gave his consent to send me to Washington on Sunday morning. He packed my baggage, purchased my ticket and put me aboard a special train. When the train left 30th Street Station, my heart was praying so loud, I could not hold my head up. I never heard such intercessory lamentation before. The words were so godly and sympathetic for every body and conditions throughout the world, I was spellbound and cried all the way. The passengers were so in sympathy with me, they manifested it, but I dare not utter a word to anyone. I felt more like having a prayer meeting than ever before. When I arrived in Washington, I called a cab and went to Pastor Kelsey's home. When he and his dear wife greeted me, they were amazed at the expression on my face. They knew how lovely my home life was. They took courage and asked me what had happened. I told them how God had blessed my soul to enter into this divine fellowship with him, how the attacks of the enemy were rained upon me from everywhere and I felt it was more than I could bear. But they are blessed with the spirit of consoling God's people.

When they told what the Lord said in His Word concerning "living godly," it oiled the wheels of trust in my soul, it stirred the gift that was within me to press forward for God even if I died. The sun was shining bright, the birds were singing, the trees were in bloom; the very atmosphere seemed to send out a welcome to my soul. The tent would seat over a thousand. When we walked under the canvas, I heard rain falling upon it like hail. I asked the pastor if he heard it, he said he did not, but he felt the presence of God in his whole body, even his legs were saying, Amen. That evening he presented me to the people; as soon as the Lord led me in prayer, two sinners came forward and fell at the altar. God saved them and the soul saving feast started. I am unable to tell you in English language how great the presence of the Lord was with me, but He worked.

So many sinners were saved we had nowhere for the seekers. I opened the prayer service on Sunday night, by Thursday of the next week, sixty souls had been saved. I was so amazed, I told the Lord if he sent Bishop Mason before the week closed, I would be confident and satisfied to work for Him, regardless of what the future presented.

The next morning, at ten o'clock, Bishop Mason called, he was at the Pennsylvania Station in Washington, D.C., enroute to the Pittsburgh conference. The pastor rushed to the station and related to him how God had sent spiritual bread to the city. Not only that but, He had supplied every financial need. Bishop Mason prayed in the station and sent him back with the message for me to "Keep on Praying", the outpour would be greater. In fourteen days, the Lord saved "ninety-five souls." A few weeks thereafter, Pastor Kelsey baptized nearly all of those converts in the Potomac River and a large group of them joined his church. Then Pastor Kelsey and his wife told Bishop Mason, God's hands were upon me. It was their desire to see the Lord's work carried on in my life, they did not want the prayer ministry abused, nor my life crushed. Undoubtedly, what they said, touched his heart concerning me.

Late one night, a telephone call came from Pastor Carr stating, Bishop Mason wanted me to meet him in Baltimore, Maryland, the next afternoon. This was another battle for me; the devil told me that Bishop Mason wanted to rebuke me as others had done. That was a miserable night, I did not sleep, I could not turn back into the world. O! this was more than I could bear.

I was so excited and nervous, my husband was afraid to drive his car to Baltimore. One of the brothers carried us.

When we arrived in Baltimore, I was so weak in my body they had to lead me into the church where Bishop Mason was waiting. I trembled like someone who had a chill. Bishop Mason showed a great concern, he wanted to know if I was ill in my body. After Elder Dabney related the story to him, he understood the situation in every detail. Like a father, he drew near unto me and took my hand, and the Lord led him out in prayer. I could hear my soul saying, "all the days of my appointed time I will wait until my change comes."

Then he read the Scripture: "yea everyone who lives in godly in Christ Jesus shall suffer persecution." He told me not to pay any attention to the devil and his attacks, but to press forward, God had greatly overshadowed and blessed me with the spirit of prayer like unto his ministry. He told me it was his long, long prayer request answered. He realized he was growing older; he could not carry the spirit of prayer on the other side with him. He had prevailed with the Lord to put it upon some of his children in the Gospel.

It came to pass, everywhere I went, the Lord confirmed His work by saving over a hundred souls, in each revival.

All nations met me. Many came because of that wicked report the devil branded me with in the beginning. As the time passed on they tried to contaminate Bishop Mason's mind with these same evil thoughts, but he rebuked them sharply for their carnal minds and unbelief in God. He told them the Son of God was branded with the same thing. The revival fire broke out; the spirit of the Lord groaned in the very depth of my soul. I could hear the Lord telling me continually: I am going to bless you more. This blessing shall become greater. As we met together, there was no discrimination, no denomination, no class, color nor creed. Then the Lord made known unto me what He said when He blessed my soul; all nations should come and pray with me while I was praying. There was a deep concern in my soul and a righteous desire to see all of God's people together; not worshipping in one building, of course, but that they should be united together in Word and in purpose; that we would all speak the same thing and walk by the same rule.

Whereas we would be able to do constructive kingdom building and convince the sinner that there is something better than merely living in the world separated from God. When I call your attention to the mountain of prayer and the Christian growth; it inspires my hope of knowing of a truth, those who walk with God do not decrease in value, but they increase, as they learn their daily lesson in the school of knowledge and wisdom from God. Too much cannot be said concerning spiritual progressiveness in consecration and prayer. Preaching is essential, it always has been. The Gospel is the power of God unto salvation unto everyone that believes.

No soul can hear without the preacher, he cannot administer God's ordinances and law nor is he able to feed the flock of God, unless he has been sent by God. Teaching is necessary; heaven is won in no other way. The Bible must be taught and obeyed for the salvation of our children, and our children's children, depends upon the correct teaching of the Bible. It is a treasure which can only be unlocked by the art of teaching; in order to teach, the tutor must know his native alphabet, above all, his spiritual guide book. But one God heard—answered prayer, will explore, undermine, root up and shake up the entire universe.

It will undermine the natural foundation of individual minds; it will place their feet on the solid rock. It will make a way for the Gospel minister. It opens the ground for "His Gospel to plow" the Word. It will send the Word piercing through stony hearts; it will sail across the ocean faster than a plane can go; it will take the hand of a lost soul and unite it with the hands of our lovely Savior.

One day Bishop Mason sent me to Los Angeles, California at the request of Bishop Crouch, the pastor of Thirty-third and Crompton Streets Church. He and his dear wife, made it possible for all nations to come and pray with me in that great revival. The meeting was so great, he wired Bishop Mason and my husband to come at once and behold the glory of the Lord. While Bishop Mason was there, he met a friend, Miss Faye Bress. She told him there was a longing in her heart to meet a woman after the old biblical type of prayer, as there was during the days of yesteryear, when the gospel fire burned in Los Angeles and stirred the world. He invited her to visit the services at Crompton Street on Sunday afternoon. I did not know she was interested in the type of woman that I am, nor the work I am engaged in. As a general rule people do not appreciate a woman who prays always. They rather class her with what they call the back number.

I left Los Angeles the next day for Philadelphia, Bishop Mason felt so sorry for me. He requested Miss Bress to send me a letter of greetings to comfort my heart when I arrived home. I received the letter; it encouraged and lifted my spirit. Miss Bress is an unusual type, she loves God with all her heart. She is a student of Scripture, a Christian lady, with an appealing personality, she is full of good work, but she never likes for anyone to give her credit for anything.

When I went to Norfolk, Virginia to pray, Pastor Williams, his dear wife and brother and sister Raddick were glad for me. But it seemed as though I was like John when he was put out on the Isle of Patmos. I did not appeal to some of the people. They were looking for a tall, stout, old woman; when they found out I was small in stature, they were very much displeased, but the Lord convinced them it was not in the age or size. He sent a prayer revival and stirred the city. When God spoke to Samuel, he was very young, but this did not hinder the manifestation from being revealed unto the priest. Many times individuals turn away a prayer answered blessing because the representative fails to meet the public ideal and approval.

The Lord told me if I would go to church at four o'clock each morning and pray, He would show me His glory in the morning time. I was under such a burden for souls to be delivered, Miss Bress felt it in Los Angeles and took it upon herself to send me a special delivery letter every other day. I answered each one, I tried to express my feelings, the obligation of the work I was doing and the sacrifice I had to make in order to please God in this prayer life and ministry. I had no idea I would ever see my name on the headlines of papers and magazines, neither had it entered my mind once that Miss Bress would publish excerpts from my personal correspondence. The Lord led her, I say it was the Lord.

I have every right to believe it was His divine plan for her to send this Gospel unto the many anxious inquirers who were languishing, conversing over what God did for Peter and John and the church in the early days. But they thought all of the praying people were dead and the Gospel was suffering for prayer warriors, in a day like this.

Miss Bress relates the story of how God moved upon her after she had read my letters. He told her to make carbon copies, send them to each pastor and request them to read it to their congregation.

She did not do this alone; she called her friends together, miss Serby, Miss Stover and Miss Davis, who are Bible School teachers. They decided it was too good and too impressive to keep in Los Angeles; they would contact Mr. and Mrs. Moore, who are publishers of tracts and papers and see if they could make arrangements to have this carbon letter published in some of the Christian magazines and papers.

Mrs. Moore contacted the Editor of the Pentecostal Evangel and his staff. They decided to publish the article under the name." It stirred up so much interest, they requested the article to be made in tract form. I did not know anything about it until one night when I went to church, after I had returned to Los Angeles on my second trip. I found on my chair an Evangel and the tract. When I read it, I almost collapsed. I told Miss Bress I knew my enemies would rail upon me greater than ever before. She only said, "Darling the mouth of the Lord has spoken and is has come to pass; it has gone too far for me to call it back."

As a result, more than three million letters are in my possession from all parts of this world. Many other noted magazines and Christian papers published the same article, which has caused this great Christian prayer publicity.

So many inquiries have been received for information concerning what I did to contact God: and what it means to pray through, that I am writing this book for no other purpose than to let you know what it means.

In all of my dealings, Jesus is the center of attraction; no place, person or thing shall be magnified in my life. I shall glory in the cross of Jesus. Humble is the way that leadeth unto everlasting life; at His feet shall be the highest place my soul shall go. I have found it to be the pinnacle for His children. All exhortations, elevation and honor will be bestowed upon each individual who will learn this one lesson, "humble is the way."

CHAPTER VII

California Trip Ends

After I had traveled extensively, Bishop Crouch called me back to Los Angeles, California; there was a great demand for my prayer ministry. This was the greatest outpour I had ever witnessed; the Lord saved eight hundred and ninety-six souls and thousands were healed of all manner of diseases. He sent the finance to help the church, pastor and the poor. He also made them a great blessing unto me. It seemed as if every nationality on the Pacific coast fellowshipped with me in this prayer meeting. They came from all parts of the country just to pray.

The Editor of the Pentecostal Evangel, Stanley Howard Frodsham, was my guest from Springfield, Missouri. It was there we had all night prayer meetings each week. It was like heaven. His stay was precious, his counsel was encouraging; it was a glorious fellowship as my husband was also my guest at this time. One night a group of Christian workers and ladies visited our services. There were three evangelists in the group: Miss Jeanette Jones and her coworker, Mrs. Esther Halverson, from Orange, California. Miss Jones was afflicted in her body.

She heard the announcement for all night prayer, availed herself of this opportunity and came. At this time, we entered into a season of fasting and prayer for ninety days and nights. Poland had been invaded. She gave me a note which informed me of her illness. The Lord told me to tell her if she would avail herself of the opportunity, and make this sacrifice and go through seventy-two hours each week, He would heal her body completely. Her congregation and family opposed because of her condition, but she obeyed God. The first two weeks she gained six pounds. When the prayer ended her body was completely healed. She is a living example of that great prayer meeting the Lord gave in Los Angeles, California.

The time came when I had to leave California for Philadelphia. It was the desire of each one that I should go away in seclusion for a rest. I had labored faithfully for five years; thousands of souls had been saved and many pastors' hearts made glad because of the spiritual and material benefits the Lord had sent them. While enroute home, I asked the Lord if He would give me the privilege and strength to pray for this war torn destructive day to close. He told me I could if I gave my boy as a sacrifice without grieving. I told Him, let it be so. On Friday morning when my son met me at North Philadelphia Station, he presented me his greetings from Uncle Sam.

He had just graduated from Pennsylvania State College as Professor of English. One afternoon I went to church, and the Lord asked me what the people were going to do while I was on my vacation. I was amazed; I knew I needed a rest but did not want to displease Him. I told Him if he wanted me to remain in Philadelphia in a prayer meeting to make it known to me by sending other nations to worship with us at once. I knew this would be a great manifestation, for at this time the Christian people were far apart in this city, so far as nationalities worshipping together is concerned. The next night three foreigners came from Washington, D.C. I could not understand their language; they did not understand me. We greeted each other with a hand shake and the power of the Lord fell upon us.

The following night nine individuals came; five different nationalities made up this group. On the third night fourteen came. From then on our church was so overcrowded with other nations, our members did not have any place in the building. I made myself satisfied to pray in Philadelphia. The meeting became so great Miss Jones, Miss Bress, Miss Davis, Mrs. Halverson and Miss Jenkins came from Los Angeles, California to pray with me. When Miss Jones arrived, she was stirred because Philadelphia did not know I was praying for everybody everywhere.

The Lord touched her heart to have my work broadcast. I did not know anything about this until one day I entered the church building and found technicians working, driving nails and making a terrible noise. I was displeased with the disturbance because the people were praying. I requested information concerning their authority. They told me they had orders to put in wires for a broadcast which would be there on Sunday night. I was confident they had made a mistake. The man took a paper out of his pocket and asked me if I knew Mrs. E.J. Dabney. I said yes, he said, she will be the principal speaker on the broadcast. I knew then, Miss Jones and Mrs. Halverson were responsible, therefore I begged him to forgive me.

On the third Sunday in February, "Nineteen hundred and forty-two," we rendered our first broadcast over Station WDAS. God gave the program, we never beg; I live by faith each week. It is encouraging to know how successful this work has been through the prayer ministry over the air. It keeps our church building crowded, the sick healed and many souls are saved.

When the people of the Lord came to the mission and found us lifting up Jesus, they were delighted. My husband is an eloquent speaker, a very humble man. The Lord has blessed him in an unusual way in preaching the Gospel; he never gets excited, he is a man of very few words, he never rushes ahead to do anything without consulting God. When he preaches and teaches the Word, the power and demonstrations are manifested.

It is remarkable the unlimited flow of words he has at his command. This is not just manifested on Sunday or some special occasion, but whenever he opens his mouth he presents words charged with the power of God. He does most of the preaching in my prayer revivals. All nationalities enjoy him as he knows how to deal with everybody. His greatest conversation is held in the pulpit. No need for anyone to think because he is quiet and gentle that anything passes his keen scrutiny in the Garden of Prayer. He is a real shepherd. The people marvel at his wisdom; many call him the young Charles E. Tindley. No one ever feels strange in this church.

When we were overcrowded, Elder Dabney was grieved because he was unable to make it comfortable for me to minister unto the helpless. He prayed and God answered his prayers.

CHAPTER VII

A New Day Dawns

One evening a group of business people visited the services. They beheld the glory of God manifested unto His people. It was a hot evening, the sick, the afflicted and sinners had crowded the building to hear the Word of the Lord. The building was not properly ventilated, in other words, there were conveniences. The guest felt sorry for me, dying on my feet, praying for the people day and night in a place like that.

They decided among themselves, it was a disgrace to Christianity to permit me to demonstrate such unselfish love unto everyone without any consideration. People were coming from all parts of the world, Syria, Africa, China, India, Australia, England and other parts of the globe. They felt sorry for me and thought something should be done. They called Bishop Mason and told him they were disgusted with the conditions under which I was laboring in that neighborhood and building simply because no one put himself out of the way to help me. They asked him if he would object if they purchased a place for my husband and me. He granted them the privilege to do whatever the Lord led them to do for me. I take this time to make it very definite and clear. Friends, those of all nationalities and denominations, who love the truth, made us a present of the church of granite, which is the Garden of Prayer. The members of our congregation did not know anything about it.

When Bishop Mason found that God had given this beautiful church, he was kind and presented a check also. He always prays for the Lord to give me some of His "Royal Bounties."

Sometimes when people present a gift, it is something which carries with it a lifetime burden. In order that you may receive first-hand information and a clear picture of THE GARDEN OF PRAYER, permit me to give you a detailed description of it and its value. It is valued at one hundred and seventy-five thousand dollars and it is fully equipped.

It is a large, picturesque building, built of granite, bordering three streets and through seven huge swinging doors with old English hinges, you may enter the church from the street. The doors are open twenty-four hours daily. There is a large "Neon Sign" on the Northeast corner of the building, in old rose and green letters, "THE GARDEN ON PRAYER." The seating capacity of the church is twenty-five hundred. There are blue velvet cushioned pews valued at ten thousand dollars, a beautiful pipe organ valued at ten thousand dollars. There are two upright pianos and a baby grand. The floors of the entire building are carpeted. There are large gothic windows. There is a heater with radiation of eighteen hundred cubic feet. In the belfry, we have a wonderful bell which calls the people to service. The building contains many private rooms which can be opened into one large assembly. There is a large lighted cross above the pulpit. I have three offices and a large letter department. There are sixteen efficient and competent girls, who work with me in this great prayer ministry and correspondence department.

These girls give gratuitous service as they learn a great lesson of faith. Many times there are thousands upon thousands of letters lying here waiting for postage. Sometimes the dear ones who send in for healing handkerchiefs, a word of consolation and scripture forget to send postage for a reply. There is no one sponsoring this work, it is carried on absolutely by faith and the willingness and generosity of these dear, sweet young women.

Last year we sent out *Seven million blessed handkerchiefs,* which had been anointed and prayed over for the sick and afflicted. We sent *three million* of the seven million to the foreign fields. The soldiers, the sailors, WAC's, trained nurses and missionaries who are stationed in the far away land received these and were greatly benefited.

Five thousand, one hundred and eighteen souls have been saved in this revival. Only God knows how many have been saved throughout the earth as the influence of this revival has reached everywhere. The presence of God is in this place! You can feel His presence on the sidewalk. As you enter the door, the arms of Jesus will greet you, the atmosphere is pregnant with the presence of God.

The people enjoy coming to this church because we do not permit whispering, chewing of gum or unnecessary walking during the services. The people are taught to respect God's house. No time is wasted, there is no begging, nothing goes on that will hinder or offend the presence of our lovely Jesus.

The Lord's Name must be hallowed. The reason we do not permit the people to converse with each other in the service is that it takes away that sense of consecration. There is no foolish talking, no jesting and no joking just to make the congregation laugh. There are no special seats, first come, first served. Great respect is paid unto the elderly people, great care is given unto the young, noone is slighted or molested. Because of this tender devotion manifested in this place, we have the privilege of seeing God manifest himself as He did when Peter stood by the wayside and the people were healed.

When our friends made it known they were seeking a building for us to pray in, which would represent the Gospel and Christian faith, the people were glad to do something to help lift the burden. Ministers, who are pastors of the Methodist, Baptist, Episcopal and Presbyterian churches here in Philadelphia, gave largely.

The business men and women of all nationalities put their hearts into the demand and responded largely to the call. Miss Jeanette Jones, her family, Mrs. Halverson and her coworker, gave generously to this cause; they are very dear to me. Miss Bress, my dear friend and kind sister whom the Lord used to make a way for my ministry universally, also helped in the purchase of this building.

May God bless my dear, kind Aunt Mary T. Taylor and her precious sister, Mrs. Holden, who sent checks for this. They always seek to help others and the Lord will bless them. There are others who cared for all of the business in detail; some of their names I do not recall. They wish to be remembered to you and to me as *"Just Friends"*. My dear Father in heaven knows who they are; may He bless, protect and increase each one spiritually and materially.

Undertakers Hobson R. Reynolds, his wife and brother were noted business people in the neighborhood. His wife taught in The Reynolds Junior High School. They never overlooked us because we worked in a mission. When we had only five members, Mr. Hobson Reynolds prayed with us faithfully and supported the work with his means and influence. God did not overlook nor forget his deeds of kindness. He served as Committeeman and Ward Leader in the District; he served three terms in The House of Representatives at Harrisburg, Pennsylvania and continued to climb the professional ladder. Today his has been elected and serves as Magistrate. Everyone who meets him knows he is a Christian gentleman. He prayed for the Garden of Prayer to succeed and become a Christian monument in the earth. In a recent visit to the Garden, he expressed his gratitude and thanks unto God for letting him live to see his prayers answered.

We found a real friend in Mr. C.P. White, Real Estate Broker, who made it possible for us to have a building for the Lord and Mr. S.Jones, a business man, our friend and neighbor, who always gave us his uncompromising support.

The Lord sent Mr. and Mrs. Mathais, who were Fish Dealers to care for us. When they found that we were honest and just, and the financial responsibility rested upon us, they made up their minds never to forget us. Many times through the heat and the cold, they sent their Little Daughter Helen with fresh trout from Delaware Bay. These people have watched our prayer life and today are listed among our most loyal friends.

CHAPTER IX

The Golden Treasure

One day when I was busy in the church, Satan called my attention to the pipe organ, and the large choir loft, and no leader or singers to occupy it. He told me I was still without the victory. When we worshipped on Ridge Avenue, we had a few singers who gathered at times, but there were untrained and not organized.

I knew the type of choir we should have. I knelt beside the altar and asked the Lord to send me one of the best instructors he had. He answered my request and sent Professor Alexander Harris. He received his early musical training from private tutors, which included Franklin Hoxter, the late Isaiah Hopkins and Eugene Frenchtinger at The Conservatory of Music. He finished a course in piano, organ, theory and harmony at Temple University School of Music. He is well versed in organ and Choral training. He received his bachelor's degree in 1930.

For a considerable time he served as director of Sunday School music at St. Matthew's and Mount Pisgah A.M.E. Churches.

He served as musical director and organist at Ward's Chapel and Jones' Tabernacle A.M.E. Churches. He directed the choir at Reeves Memorial Presbyterian Church.

When I observed the talent and characteristics of this young man, I remembered the encouraging correspondence Paul wrote Timothy, his son, in the Gospel.

He called his attention to the great love of God and Christian faith he found in his mother, Eunice and his grandmother, Lois. He did not hide from Timothy his candid opinion concerning the fruits of a prayerful family tree. He was very sincere in his declaration, when he

47

told him that he was confident, that the same Christian principles and qualifications had also been instilled into his life. Few parents ever take time to consider how important it is "to train up a child in the way he should go."

This is my conviction: I believe the first wise step that a young man makes is to serve the Lord, and the people—that most important step, his precious mother taught him. Youth is the most vital and important moment to instill and the only ideal time to sharpen the true principles and valuable seeds of an adult life. This must be done by the parents, especially the mother, before the child is born. Education has never produced enough power and skill to make spiritual leaders. They are born. It requires thought and a vision of the future; there must be a choice selection of the material that is put into the floor of a child's life.

Then the parents must strictly understand that they are the child's first teachers. This is a thought, worthy of consideration, in a day like this. There are parents who think it is wrong to pay attention to a child's activities. They never seek to find out just what interests the child most. This is very necessary; there is something about the personalities and characteristics in children, which if wisely observed, can readily be recognized.

Professor Harris' mother relates an incident which occurred when he was just two years old. She sent him to a music teacher to learn the scales. The boy played the Lord's Prayer and the doxology all the way through without making a mistake. His professor became so excited that he contacted her immediately and told her a genius had been born in her family. The story of his childhood is impressive; he always lived more or less to himself. He investigated and adored everything pertaining to music. He has two sisters and three brothers who seem to think that he is a God sent blessing to the family. Furthermore, the old precious family altar still remains in that home.

He relates how in the infancy of his career sometimes clouds overshadowed, but his mother prayed until the sun shone again. No one ever achieved success starting from the top. A successful life begins at the bottom level—step by step it leads upward. When we see men serving in natural battles with hardships and disappointments, we wonder why some go down in disgrace and defeat, while others rise to hone and fame. Life is a pilgrimage, while we travel, we encounter storms and hardships; sometimes we call them "school books" from which we learn our career lessons.

But this is not the only battle where men learn warfare. There is also a Christian battle in life. Every individual who enlists in the Christian army must fight against the opposing, contaminating forces of Satan and his host.

False friends who pull the cord to hinder and blind the spiritual vision of success, live in that undermining current; there are mined water and hidden nets which force the soldier of the cross, the Gospel seaman, to war with difficulties. Sometimes individuals think it is a disgrace to say a child of the Kind has to war; but this life is a battle, sometimes with the satanic forces within themselves, but then we consider the Lord's guide, which has been ruled and chartered—it is in His blueprint; "if you suffer, you shall reign."

The church is not just a cast off shelter of a deserted camp, nor is it an old log cabin, built off the road, in the backwoods of some hot, sandy desert. But it is God's saving station; it is God's sanctuary; it is the only building in the world where His children can go and find His beauty and glory in ta bountiful supply. It is His information bureau. It is heaven's laundry to whiten and prepare souls for the grand reunion over there. The fountain never closes in God's church; the fluid never dries up. The blood of Jesus has never lost its power; God's library is in his church; it is there He meets His children and satisfies their longing desires. When all other rocks crumble, quake and fall, God's church still stands as a monument with the Gospel's flag of victory and the banner of love. Then we must have qualified workers, those who have denounced the hidden things of dishonesty, who have been robed in the robe of righteousness and praise, to show forth His glory, humor and virtue unto a suffering, sick, dying world. If they are not in the church, our Jesus, commanded us to pray unto our Father in heaven, and He would be delighted to send laborers into His vineyard.

This young man is not only a genius, but he has a very unusual respect for his parents. After receiving an education through the unlimited sacrifices they made for him, he has not forgotten them in the evening of their lives. They are his companions; they are his dearest friends. He refused a family life for himself, and gave his time to make their lives comfortable, and worthwhile living.

He esteemed his ability to work in the ministry of Christ a privilege, and a blessing to suffer with the people of God. He is very humble and conservative—a man of very few words. At present he is serving on of the oldest Methodist Church Choirs in America. The church was founded by the late Honorable Richard Allen, who was noted for his humanitarian acts. This church is called Mother Bethel; it is known throughout Christendom.

He is also director and organist of the choir of fifty-one voices, and a chorus of fifty-seven voices, of our internationally known "Garden of Prayer", located on Twenty-ninth and Susquehanna Avenue, Philadelphia, Pennsylvania. Many letters of commendation are received from interested listeners to our broadcast each Sunday evening.

In many instances, the power of God is so great in the music and singing, souls are converted in the streets, in the homes, and while sitting in their automobiles. Professor Harris is a member of the local branch of the National Association of Musicians, and the Philadelphia Music Conference. After you observe a part of his family history, you will also acknowledge the fact, that all of his success is attributed to a praying mother and father, who pray for him while he serves the people, and that precious family altar.

There is no word in language to tell,
The good that you have done.
Regardless what's said, you never swell.
You shall reap in the day to come.
There is a place in the wisdom of God,
There in His cleft, you will see
The notes He taught when you were very small
Let your Faith look up to Me.
Singing is honored in heaven above;
It touches the hearts of men.
It expresses your Savior's precious love
It draws from the bondage of sin.

Your God and your parents are your theme song.
This is the secret of your success.
Lift up your head, you cannot go wrong
When you give your Lord's service your best.
God bless you for the way you work with me,
For my song with the music you gave.
May He bless and keep you, it is my plea.
May He give you strength to be brave.
Those nieces and nephews you love so dear,
Your sisters and brothers who pray for you,
With the Christian army and the Garden of Prayer
There is nothing to fear, "GO THROUGH"!
The Lord gave the Moon and Sun to shine,
This world was made by His plans,
He calls His children to come and dine
This is why He blessed your hands.
The greatest blessing you will receive
Shall be revealed after while,
When your Savior shall say He is well pleased
And greet you with a smile.
No more toiling with choirs and choruses then
Your career's victory will be won.
Gabriel's choir will sing the Alleluias and Amens,
When He shall say, well done, My son.

CHAPTER X

Material For The Palace

Pennsylvania is known as the Keystone State, and Philadelphia carries the title of The City of Brotherly Love. Among the many women who have risen to fame by their kind, humanitarian deeds and arts of charity are: Betsy Ross, Mrs. Mary E. Tribbett, Mrs. Annie L. Blackwell and Miss Marian Anderson. The name of Mrs. Harriet M. Ways cannot be forgotten. She was born in the lovely State of Virginia; came to Philadelphia when she was young, opened a school and taught Beauty Culture. She was an invalid for five years, not knowing anything about healing through prayer, but a good missionary related the story and made it so sweet, Mrs. Ways, accepted divine healing. She was an active church worker, and had an experience of how to deal with individuals.

The Lord put it upon her heart to have cottage meetings in the city. The prayer revival fire broke out, and the Lord manifested Himself in such a great way, the Church of God in Christ in Philadelphia sprang out of this. She never accepted the idea of pastoring the people, but when the church went through a great persecution, she held the people together by prayer until Bishop Mason sent Elder O.T. Jones to pastor them. Her labor is invaluable. She was Church Mother for many years. Her prayerful influence and work assisted many struggling pastors during the depression. She called the praying women together and prayed two days monthly in each church. This encouraged the pastors and congregations to lift up their heads and pray through. I had the privilege of waiting before the Lord with her during those precious hours. Our records show she was not only a spiritual blessing, but also a great material and financial help.

During this time, she gave the pastors three thousand, three hundred and nineteen dollars. She gave the churches two thousand, two hundred and ten dollars. This free will offering came in while she taught the daughters how to contact the Lord in prayer. Thousands of individuals were healed. Work was very scarce at that time, but in answer to her prayer, God sent employment and lifted the heads of many who were despondent. She sent a prayer call to all prayer warriors who each morning from seven until eight met the Lord in prayer.

"Two Watches." She prayed until the Lord lifted the band of depression and sent the people to work. Today the Lord has opened the way for her. She is the honored Supervisor for the Women's Christian Department, in the Church of God in Christ, for the State of Pennsylvania. One of the women who worked in that great prayer battle, Ida B. Martin, has become her assistant in this field of endeavor, to lift up fallen humanity in the Name of Jesus.

The influence and confidence of that prayer still live in Philadelphia. Many of those women whom she taught how to pray are noted leaders and prayer warriors today.

They have God's approval; some of them are serving faithfully in the war area, where the Word of God and much prayer is needed. "Kingdoms may fall, and generations may change, but the work done by this "Queen of Prayer" shall never be forgotten.

A PRAYER

Dedicated to my friends who gave me the church.
Dear God, thank you for watching over me
Through the days of yesteryear.
All of those blessings you hid from me
Now you have presented them, Father Dear.
Thank you for each friend You gave,
Who purchased this building for Thee.
Ridge Avenue would have sent me to my grave,
But your dear children rescued me.
Bless each one who went ahead,
With business of this kind;

Answer each request they have made,
Unto Thee at any time.
Jesus Savior, pilot these,
Encourage and lead the way.
Precious Father, grant their pleas,
In Jesus' name I pray.
Bless all of Thy children everywhere,
In this dark hour of distress;
Administer the strength and rebuke the fear;
Go with us through this test.
It is not because you do not care,
The sacrifice and lives we risk,
But Satan tempted and we went astray,
Please forgive in a day like this.
Whereve4r the sick may be, Dear God,
Have mercy if You please;
Do not forget the lame and the blind, Be merciful unto these.
The blood of Thy Son still atones,
His blood still has its power.
O bless, Dear Father, deliver your own,
Send us your refreshing shower.
I come quickly to Thy mercy seat,
To the altar you made for me;
O! Praise the Lord, my heart, my soul;
The Lord is here with Thee.

CHAPTER XI

Wisdom In The Prayer Cabinet

"Fret not thyself because of evil doers; neither be thou envious against the workers of iniquity; they shall soon be cut down like the green grass and wither as the green herb. Trust in the Lord, do good, and verily thou shalt be fed. Delight thyself also in the Lord, and he shall give thee the desires of thine heart. Commit they ways unto the Lord; trust also in Him, and He will bring it to pass." Psalm 37:1-5.

To work in the divine ministry of Jesus, some leaders are blessed to have the material they need at hand. I never have been able to walk into the streets, and find efficient workers standing on the street corners, waiting to be hired in this prayer battle. No one ever rang my doorbell and requested a position. This is very strange as people seek opportunities to work elsewhere; but in this work, seldom can you find competent, efficient Christian workers, who will assume the responsibility, and work wholeheartedly, looking unto Jesus for their reward. Maybe it is because the people realize what it means to work hard all day, and all night, trying to help inspire souls to accept the upper bright world.

The way seemed very cloudy, but I knew the Lord had plenty of wisdom reserved in "His Prayer Cabinet," for those who had the key to fit the lock. When my work became universally noted, the hearts of the people were stirred throughout the world. *The Pentecostal Evangel,* and other noted magazines, and Christian papers published the article, *"What It Means to Pray Through."* God sent the word and stirred the people. It awakened the hearts of the people in such a great way, many of the Editors told me they were utterly amazed.

We know it was God, nothing is too hard for Him. The first article and publication brought thirty-five thousand letters; this does not include postcards, telegrams and cables. My task was very heavy. I had to answer each letter personally and catalogue names and addresses. It was too great a responsibility with my prayer ministry. I considered the advice Moses' family gave him. I knew it would be better if I had some one with the spirit of God who would serve faithfully and work with my program. This is a very lonely day, much good can be accomplished through letter writing.

Many times I receive letters from young men and women who are despondent; they are students, but disappointment and contaminating forces blind their vision; they become discouraged and dissatisfied with their own life. At times, mothers and fathers who are brokenhearted, find their way and consolation through correspondence from this office. Not only those who have never been able to visit the Garden of Prayer, but also thousands upon thousands of others who desire help come each night. I am unable to give a personal interview, for I must stay with God, but through writing, I am able to send good news and glad tidings from the Bible unto many benighted souls.

Letters are my personal friends; they are my comfort; I do not permit even a request to be cast aside or thrown into the waste basket, regardless of how cheap the paper may be upon which the request is written. An individual who desires something from God is the author. I always think, what would Jesus do if He received a note, a letter or a card from me?

One night I walked out to my prayer mountain; I conversed with the Lord very definitely concerning the work and the office. I asked Him to consider my responsibility and send me a young Christian woman who was competent, efficient and consecrated to work in the letter department.

I requested Him to make a choice of her qualifications; I was confident whoever He sent would not be a burden maker, but a burden lifter. He answered my request. He sent Miss Leta Ashley. When I met her, I knew she was an answer to my prayer. She was a Christian, active in church work. She had completed a commercial course in high school. Her mother had given her a special course in bookkeeping under private tutors. When she graduated, her ambitions led her to aspire unto higher ideals.

Satan never permits a real child of God to go through life without experiencing tests and piercing trials. He afflicted her mother's body; she was an invalid for five years. Miss Ashley did not cast her mother aside, when she came to that place where she felt the hand of Providence had to work, she remembered those hands and the vessel who labored for her before she was born. She gave due respect unto her mother and made a living for her until the Lord called her from labor unto reward. Then she was left alone with one sister who is a Beauty Culturist. She is a Christian young woman and well loved.

Miss Ashley's life was quite blank, but the Lord gave her a very honest friend, and God Mother, in the person of Sara Kendall Cunningham. Little Sara was very young, but the Lord blessed her with His Word. She had a deep concern for everybody, especially the young people.

Her father and mother were dear armour bearers and friends to me when I went through the covenant for three years. Her mother felt sorry for me. Many souls were led to the mission because of the information she gave them. She instilled those motherly, Biblical qualities into little Sara. She was able to relieve Miss Ashley of many responsibilities. A few years thereafter, affliction seized Miss Ashley's body. One night, she dialed her radio, and there was the Garden of Prayer broadcasting; she heard the prayer for everybody, everywhere. She decided to visit the church. When she entered the door the Lord Jesus met her, broke the fetters and chains that bound, and restored her health completely.

She saw me struggling, and realized she was born to work in the Lord's vineyard. She offered her service help lift the burden. We found that she was born for this type of work; it is a gift rather than mere education.

Christian letter writing is not new, but is as old as creation. It pleased our Father to give men wisdom and knowledge to write; there is something skillful and outstanding about it; wherever a message is directed if delivered, it will convey its meaning.

It not only has been used to convey natural meanings but our Father also used it to speak unto rulers in ancient times. When the

King tried to molest the consecrated vessels it displeased the Lord. He did not send a special officer to arrest him; He did not call him on the phone; He did not call a special church meeting; He just stretched out His hand and wrote on the wall in the King's guest chamber. His writing caused so much trouble, nobody was able to enjoy the feast. The wise men became distressed and illiterate; their education did not mean a thing when the Lord id the writing.

Daniel prayed through into the Lord's glory; He had a great feast prepared for him in the servants' quarters directly from heaven. His God was by his side; not only that, but also this was the time when the Lord decided to make know unto man what it really means to exalt God and honor Him daily. Daniel was not invited to be one of the guests at the King's banquet; he was not insulted, nor cast aside because there was no card with name engraved. The entertaining hose, Belshazzar, failed to see God, but the royal blood was flowing in Daniel's veins. Many individuals permit their wealth, office and high standing to blind their vision, and send "self-righteousness and the spirit of pride" into their hearts which leads them to ignore individuals who are living for God, and His Kingdom. Not only does the seat of pride predominate, but there is an evil which makes some people isolate and forget that servant whom the Lord has put His approval upon. Daniel was not only a servant of the Lord, but he honored God; whatever he undertook regardless of how great the responsibility or how small the task, he always consulted his God. Then his prayer of thanksgiving is outstanding and intelligent. Sometimes we wonder why God honored Daniel in this manner. I am confident the Christian reader will understand what it means to value the real source of prayer. I do not think it is wise to wait until trouble drives a soul to call on God; a wise individual is one who seeks to stay with the Lord and His commandments continuously.

When you walk with God and all of your ways please Him, heaven's etiquette will be in your heart. Should the hours arrived, when the Lord needs someone to witness before the Kings and rulers, He will consider that child who spends most of his time with Him, and the only one He can trust. I can see Daniel's praying feet ascending hills and mountains;

by walking out so far with the Lord, he was on the pinnacle spiritually speaking, although in the natural he was in the helps' room.

There is something in even the look of a prayer warrior the world has never been able to explain. I can see those high-minded men bowing to that soldier. When the banquet bells rang, and the whistles blew, the music played welcoming the King's guest. They had not given Daniel a cup of soup, nor a saltine cracker, but now he was perfectly welcome to help himself to any of the food he desired, but he did not have a desire to defile himself with the King's meat. When the Kind saw Daniel's consecrated humble face and the glory of God shining upon it, he lifted his tear-filled eyes and waiting eagerly to hear what was the interpretation of the inscription. All of those wise men and royal guests paid attention to Daniel.

Thank God, he was not excited; he knew that he was the Lord's gold from His prayer cabinet. They had not considered him, but now they looked upon him as a wise man, and they were ready to give him enough riches to carry him through life in luxury and splendor. I am elated to know he refused all of their offers. He was rich; His Father in heaven had all that he needed. He was very intelligent and sweet in his manner when he said unto them: "Let they gifts be unto thyself, I will read the writing. My Father sent me here for this purpose, and if there is any overtime my Father in heaven will pay me." He had taken a long course in the school of suffering, he advanced in the college of hard knocks; he received his degree in trusting God, he was as gentle as a lamb. As soon as he focused his eyes on the writing on the wall, his Father in heaven removed the curtains which hid the interpretation from the wise and prudent and revealed unto His servant.

Not only was the interpretation and message delivered unto the Kind, but the Lord stood by Daniel and proved that he was telling the truth by fulfilling his sayings.

When John was placed on the Isle of Patmos, he prayed through; as soon as he went out into the spirit, immediately the spirit of the Lord came upon him, lifted him, and commanded him to write letters to those who were leaders, and to the seven churches of Asia Minor. Not only unto that dispensation were his letters beneficial, but also in a day like this, when we observe the contents of those letters which were written many years ago, our hearts and souls are stirred.

I wonder what we do if it were not for the scrolls, documents, and parchments which were written by the holy men of old as God moved upon them through the Holy Ghost.

I adore Apostle Paul's letters; he was gifted to put on paper what he had in his heart. His letters are compiled and written with such simplicity that they remind me of the individual who has a conversational touch with a personal interview. Never has letter writing been so much in demand as in a day like this. The generals, the majors, soldiers and sailors, the WAC's, WAVES and SPARS and all who are engaged in this universal conflict, are encouraged and inspired through writing. Therefore, when a young man or woman accepts the office, and gives his talent to write unto the ends of the earth, he has accepted an important call from God, and great shall be his reward. No one can write for an organization or society greater than Christian publication and the ministry of prayer.

It is true, I observe the contents of each letter personally. It is Miss Ashley, who has catalogued and filed with a card system, thousands, yes, millions of names and addresses from all parts of the world. She has a great intellectual ability and much experience. She has an appealing personality, is gentle and conservative, perfectly honest in every detail.

It may not be your task to go
Into countries far away;
You can help the wanderer at your door
You can read, write and pray.
Some of the greatest needs in the ministry today
Are for those who use their pen;
For those who are prepared in every way
To enlighten the hearts of men.
Business is a part of a Christian's life,
How lovely when one can stand
Free from self-righteousness and strife,
And supply the church demands.
It is right that a record be kept,

In heaven they have the same.
You will not be counted with those who slept
If you continue in Jesus' Name.
Writing is wisdom from above
It has been used throughout the years;
It expresses our kind Saviour's love,
It has delivered many hearts from fears.
Pray on and write, the Lord will bless,
His presence shall go with thee,
He will help you to meet every test
He will pay you for working with me.
Your aunt and sister are glad to know
You made your life worthwhile.
The staff, your friends, turn the green light Go!
Your name is on heaven's file.
Some day we shall gather over there,
In that city of your King;
You will see added starts in your crown,
You gained by using your pen.

A PRAYER
Dedicated to Mrs. Sarah Long

Our Father, bless in this distressed land.
Forgive our sins I pray.
Let us be delivered by Thy hand,
Turn death's destruction away;
Mothers and wives with broken hearts,
Are praying for peace to come?
Rebuke Satan and his fiery darts,
Please send our boys back home.
Oh, Father, stir your ministers to pray!
You gave to them the keys;
Lead them to that old way,
Humble repentance on their knees.
Bless the fields with harvest green,
The fowl, the birds and the flock,
Turn away the devourer that would destroy these,
Time our praying clock.
Bless the rulers of the law;
The children in the land.
Break the bands, lock the lion's jaw;
We will obey your commeands.

—Amen.

CHAPTER XII

The Old Fashion Church Prayer Revival

A group of ministers asked me if it were foolish for farmers and victory gardeners to send in requests for prayer for their business; No! It is not foolish. God's blessings and guidance should be requested in everything we do. A few years ago when mothers and fathers started home life with the prayer altar; the Lord not only blessed their bodies; but also their business.

They prayed over the seed, the corn, beans, peas and potatoes. Those who raised poultry for commercial purposes had an abundant success. They prayed for the cattle, butter and cream were plentiful and farming was a pleasure. I have seen as many as six and seven ears of corn on one stalk. I have counted as many as seventeen potatoes in a hill; in fact, there were so many large potatoes the medium and small ones were used for the hogs. The trees were heavy laden with delicious fruit. Individuals gathered nuts and berries by the basket. Today there are people who try to minimize this type of Christian standard and reverence unto God. But years ago those individuals found the key to a successful family life and constant prayer revivals.

Regardless how large the family circle grew, there was always an abundant supply. They shared their blessings with their neighbors, not because their friends were suffering, but they had that loving, kind spirit of Jesus in their hearts, which taught them how to consider others.

The oil never ran out, nor was the bread rationed. In those days, the church officials prepared the hearts of the people for what they called "Old Camp Meeting", or "Protracted Meeting."

Both men and women made it their business to assemble together in cottage meetings or the church house. They corrected mistakes and repented for whatever they had in their hearts that displeased God and their fellow workers. When they adjusted matters and conditions, it changed the very atmosphere in the community, in the home and the church.

They fasted and prayed, and the Lord sent His presence. The Holy Spirit was poured out in a great way, however they did not know that it was the Holy Spirit operating as we do today.

Many times, the presence of the Lord was so great upon them that they walked the aisles of the church and wrung their hands; they rejoiced and praised God out of the very depths of their soul. They requested the Lord to send "A soul redeeming meeting".

The Mothers of the church occupied the "Amen Corner". They wore long pleated dresses, beautiful white, starched and ironed aprons, slat bonnets and the old famous turban hat which is very popular today. A few feet from the "Amen Corner" was the "Mourners' Bench".

Sinners did not go there to look around, nor did they dare play or whisper in the House of God. They did not tell funny jokes or fables to make the people laugh; they were sincere in their worship. They acknowledged the glory of the Lord, and their prayers ascended unto the throne of God.

The Word of God was preached under the power of the Holy Ghost. Stony hearts of men, women and children quaked under the mighty hand of God.

The prayer revival news swept the country; it stirred the cities and towns and the regions round about. It was a glorious sight to see the people gathering from everywhere to be in that great outpour. They did not have automobiles; they used horses and buggies, ox-carts double mule teams, wagons and many came on foot. After those Christians humbled themselves unto the Lord, their prayers charged the ground for miles. Those enroute to the meeting have witnessed the presence of the Lord five and six miles away from the church building.

It was so precious they ran as fast as they could to enter that divine service. Nobody ever thought of carrying a sandwich to church. The farmers and gardeners honored the Lord, and He multiplied their increase. They did not know what it was to be in want; whenever the meeting convened they made ready to feed everybody who came.

As far as eyes could see, tables were spread with the very best food: everything was free.

Seekers who went early in the morning to the "Anxious Altar" refused to feast whit the multitude, but they went away seemingly, and agonized to find God, who was able to wash them in His blood from their sins. They buried their faces in their hands; tear drops fell on the floor.

No one told them what to say; they had to press through; they had to contact God for themselves. If they did not find the Lord the first day, no one had to beg them to return to the altar the next day. They went home, prayed all night; early the next morning they arose from that altar, went out into the fields and woods, and cried unto the Father of heaven to forgive their sins, and redeem their souls.

When the hour arrived for day session, there was no coaxing; something down in those seekers' hearts made them so hungry for salvation they were at the church door when the janitor arrived. They went immediately to the "Mourners Bench" and prayed through. May I say, they really received what they were looking for.

Sinner who visited the meetings with no intention of seeking salvation did not stay around the Christians and the House of God. They had respect for the worship place. Naturally they would have, because the Christians bestowed great honor and reverence upon the House of God.

There was something outstanding and intelligent about these meetings. When the Lord converted their souls, they were not ashamed to tell what manifestation had been granted. They saw marvelous visions; the Lord manifested Himself to them; each one had a personal experience of what the Father, the Son and the Holy Spirit was. They were so enthused, they told it in the valley and upon the mountain tops, what demonstration and manifestation they had received directly from the courts of glory.

It felt like a prayer meeting was going on. It attracted the attention of all classes, creeds and colors. There was no separation, "Big I or Little You", everybody was on the same level and it was instructive to follow the young converts as they entered into a new life for the Lord.

Great care was given to each little soul by the adult members of the church. They knew these little lives were little gospel plants in the soil of the world and the ground of the church. They were little tender trees. What I admired about the converts was, they did not rise from the prayer altar with a degree or diploma upon how to overcome temptations. They knew they had a long journey to travel. They accepted instructions and teachings from the proper sources of the church.

The parents, the home, the Sunday school and church was their ideal. They were taught to know the difference between the right and wrong. The praying women assumed the responsibility of praying for each new convert individually; they made it their daily duty.

Whenever Satan tempted that "Young soldier of the Cross," these women knew it. Sometimes they walked six and seven miles to comfort those young Christians and no sacrifice seemed to be too great for them to make. This strengthened the hearts of those girls and boys and they were taught that they could not do sinful acts and feel their Saviour's care.

A Christian farmer is a God-sent blessing; they shall ever be remembered continuously in my prayers. When farmers prayed years ago, the pestilence and plagues that came to destroy the vegetables, fruits and grain were rebuked. The children and adults lived happy and healthy lives.

I have always been a close observer of prayer and how God worked when people honored Him. Although I was very young, I admired the deep, rich color the Lord gave the grass products. I thank God for the many letters I have received from farmers and the tillers of the soil requesting prayer for their business. I want each one to know this is accepted with the Lord.

If you worship the Lord whole-heartedly, and give Him tithes of all, He will bless you abundantly. In Malachai 3:10, the Lord commands each one: "Bring ye all the tithes into the storehouse, that there may be meat in my house, and prove me now herewith, saith the Lord of hosts, if I will not open you the windows of heaven, and pour you out a blessing, that there shall not be room enough to receive it. And I will rebuke the devourer for your sakes, and he shall not destroy the fruits of your ground; neither shall your vine cast her fruit before the time in the fields, said the Lord of Hosts".

If you love the Lord and obey His commandments, treat everybody right and do that which is good, He will not only send you a material blessing, but He will send a universal "Soul-saving harvest".

Prayer is the key to the Lord's heaven door. It encourages every leader, minister and missionary when they observe the ingathering of the Lord's spiritual harvest. I believe in asking for divine guidance in everything pertaining to business and human life. I know the church plays a great part in supplying spiritual products. The home life should be esteemed very highly in a day like this. I have a request on the altar; I am praying that God will permit the time to return when the family altar will be rebuilt and restored in its rightful place in the home.

There is a great need for Christian home and family worship in this hour of distress and destruction. We cannot afford to work all day with our hands and our minds occupied, with our hearts overcrowded with the material side of life, and then expect a great universal revival to break out everywhere.

We shall have a new class and group of individuals to deal with when this destruction passes. The boys who survive will return with a different view on life. Some of them never had the privilege of listening to a prayer in the home by their father and mother. They do not know anything about the spiritual fire-side chat. Even though many of them are ungodly, it would inspire and teach them how to start life anew if they are greeted with the prayer atmosphere, which surrounds that home which has a family altar.

The Sunday School will have a wonderful opportunity to instill the principles of Christ in those despondent veterans.

I love everybody and it seems to be an honored gift and favor from the Lord, that He has bestowed upon me to deal with youth in a day like this. We have a host of young people in the Garden of Prayer. We feel the responsibility to teach and instill the word, and business principles in the lives of these young people. We have an excellent Sunday School. The pastor and I are aware of the fact that not only the adults but also children need very special training and care, therefore we make it our business to teach the junior classes. He teaches the boys and I teach the young girls. By making this sacrifice and devoting our time, we are able to report wonderful progress.

I have sixty-nine scholars in my class; they are known as Class Number Four. They are a group of refined, well-trained, sober, sensible spiritual girls. These girls are training for different business careers. Above all they are students of the Bible. Many of them spend their week-ends in the church fasting and praying. On Saturday evenings they have a chance to deliver the Word of the Lord. This does not make them preachers, but it is essential for them to express themselves before those with whom they have to deal. I know thy are young their ideas and ambitions cannot be limited, but they must have an experienced tutor and leader, one who knows youth problems and understands how to solve them in meekness and sincerity. These girls also make up the chorus which renders the sweet music in the Garden of Prayer. They are the faithful Junior Ushers. Whenever an auxiliary in the church needs an efficient secretary, they always select one from Class Number Four. Baby Rosette Johnson, the daughter of Mr. and Mrs. George Johnson, is the little usher for Class Number Four. Each Sunday morning she is dressed in her white uniform and gloves, white socks and black patent leather shoes. She is just three years old, but she prays and asks the Lord to bless her in her work.

Chapter XIII

A Peep Into The Revival Scenes

By Miss J. Jones

Many people think in this modern age, in which we live, the old-fashion prayer warriors and meetings are long forgotten. One night in May, we had an Eastern guest in our home. We knelt in the living room crying out to God for a deeper, closer walk with Jesus. We felt the tug of the Spirit at our hearts' door calling us unto the ministry of fasting and prayer. I shall never forget it. Rising from my knees, briny tears had coursed down my cheeks. I walked over to the window and stood gazing on the handiwork of God. The snow-capped mountain in the distance, the field of orange and avocado groves surrounding us and stretched out for miles before us, this was a beautiful sight indeed.

Almighty God was talking to my heart about fasting and prayer. It was at the midnight hour a few days later that after driving forty miles at the conclusion of our service, we entered into a holy sanctuary in Los Angeles, at Thirty-third and Compton Streets. The lights were dim and the glory of God was in that place. We heard a sweet voice of a woman praying, "everywhere, bless everywhere, Lord! Send the rain!" Then peeled forth the strains of that song, "I need Thee, O, I need Thee, every hour I need Thee". Listen! What's this I hear? Prayfully sung and floating through the air, it sounded like the echo of angels at the lone hour of midnight, "Jesus, lead me, lest I stray, Gently lead me all the way; I am safe when by Thy side, I would in Thy love abide."

Where? What is this you are talking about? Come! My friend, enter with me into the Garden of Prayer. The platform was crowded with men, and below the platform, filling the entire front of the church, were assembled the women in the solemn assembly of "prayer". Holy hands were lifted heavenward, the cries of God's warriors on the battle field, while friend and foe were sleeping, was "Everywhere! Everywhere! Bless everywhere, Lord". Just then a gust of heavenly wind swept through the building. Voices blended together in divine harmony sounded as the noise of many waters. Lord exclamations of hallelujahs and praises arose as an incense unto God.

Hush! Is that from heaven? Can it be that some instrument is so yielded to the Lord that their chords are touched with heaven? A "Holy hush" swept over the "Garden"; the perfume of heaven was scenting the atmosphere, not a sound to be heard while this melody filled with notes only known in heavenly contact, peeled forth in holy, angelic grandeur. Then, without a discord, all voices united in a heavenly anthem. Such melody, such singing and yet not a word uttered. The words of that song became a reality, "There will be singing up in heaven, such as you never heard."

No talking, no whispering, no disturbance, but at this point a friend kneeling beside me said, "This is heaven". Were it possible to go to sleep in this atmosphere, you would declare upon awakening that you entered heaven.

Another scene! Unitedly the throng under the control of the Holy Spirit entered into soul agony. Such groans, such moans, such weeping, such labour, such agonizing, "Spare Thy people! O Lord, spare Thy people." Everybody was remembered in prayer. Those in every capacity that could be named: in the religious world, the hospitals, staff, doctors, nurses and patients, judges, attorneys, mayors, governors, presidents, kings, rulers at home and abroad; those on the battlefield, their wives, children, parents, brothers and sisters, the ships at sea, captains sail.

What is coming now? A cloud burst, another wave of glory! Our precious, humble little sister Dabney, who is seated on the floor in the centre, just below the platform, is illuminated with the glory of God. She speaks saying, "Children, get ready, the Special is coming; Jesus the Physician, is arriving with His healing basket, filled with new eyes, new hearts, new organs; tell Him what you need. Give Him your troubles; Jesus the Fetter Breaker, is on His way," then she cried, "Quick! Get ready!" Then the announcement, "Jesus is here". By this time you feel the prostrating power of God. People are slain here and there under the power of God; in this atmosphere we have seen the blind receive their sight, those that were brought in dying condition made whole. Cancers, tumors, growths and afflictions of all kinds and descriptions are buried in the "Healing Waters that rise high in the "Garden of Prayer". Coming to the close of one of these "All nights" spent with Jesus, the saints arise looking like so many electric lights. They are so charged and illuminated with the glory of God. You should hear their testimonies as they tell of what Jesus did when He passed by that night.

Dear reader, I have tried to depict to you just one of the all nights of prayer that my co-worker, Sister Esther C. Halverson and I attended when Sister Dabney was in Los Angeles. In this meeting you will find all races and denominations represented. The tenth of June, Nineteen hundred and forty-one a "World-wide call to prayer" was made by Sister Dabney. She stated, "I will be fasting three days and nights out of each week abstaining from food and water; I do not ask you to do this, but I do ask you to pray."

It is astonishing to witness the number that responded to this "Fast", and I for one, am glad to report the sustaining grace of Jesus, as He gloriously carried me through. I feel better now than I have in years; because I have been healed from two organic deformities. Sister Dabney is now at her home in Philadelphia, praying in a days ago reporting how wonderfully God is working in great revival which has lasted for over three years and a half in her husband's church. We received letters a few that place.

Our Little Sister carries on an "Unseen Revival" daily through the medium of correspondence. Each letter receives her personal attention; she prays over the handkerchiefs and the miracles recorded in this manner are stupendous. I have even known her to send telegrams and cablegrams to those on the verge of suicide. She counts no effort too great to save a soul from hell, and to encourage the Christian traveler on his way.

In a recent letter received from her she writes: "The States are spending billions to free the people from destruction, why should I not give all that I have to help God's poor people who are suffering for the need of a conversation with the Lord? Does the revival continue in Los Angeles?" Oh, yes! The Prayer Warriors are still fighting. Sister Faye Bress, the lady to whom Sister Dabney sent the letters that have stirred the world through the tract on, *"What It Means to Pray Through"* is still faithful at her post. Remember, dear co-workers, prayer lives on.

In January, Nineteen hundred and forty-four, the Lord sent me to Philadelphia to visit the Garden of Prayer. It is wonderful to behold the marvelous work the Lord is doing in that city. The cordial welcome they bestowed upon me will be remembered as long as I live. Not only the members of the Garden of Prayer, but the friends of Radio land. May God bless each one, Amen.

Chapter XIV

The House Of The Lord

"The gold for the things of gold, and the silver for the things of silver, and for all manner of work to be made by the hands of artificers." And whom then is willing to consecrate his service this day unto the Lord?

The house of the Lord always presents a hearty welcome when it is kept immaculate. When the people enter the Lord's house to pray and worship they feel better when they know care has been given. Because the church doors are open unto all; some people like to kneel and pray; it is gratifying when one can feel comfortable. When we moved into our new church I asked the Lord to give us someone to care for it. I knew whoever assumed that responsibility would have to have salvation and business ability. He answered my prayer and sent a very precious young woman, Miss Julia Connor.

When she graduated from Statesville High School in North Carolina, she had great ambition to achieve an intellectual and spiritual career.

Her dear parents sent her to Brenard College at Chester, South Carolina. She was very successful. She studied there for two years and entered Bible school in North Carolina. It was so interesting she completed her studies and taught in summer Bible Schools. She came to Philadelphia two years ago and joined the Garden of Prayer.

Her Christian life and intellectual ability was so outstanding, I gave her a place on our "Secretarial Staff". She had a part time position elsewhere. The defense workers whose positions prevented them from attending evening church services appreciated our daily open door.

The sick, the afflicted, both young and old, love to go there to pray and rest.

Our pastor and the official board observed how the Lord had touched the hearts of the people to come to church daily and pray, they suggested, it would be wise to have an efficient Bible teacher present each day to encourage the hearts of the visitors. The telephone keeps one busy all day praying and speaking words of consolation unto the heavy-hearted. Miss Connor fills this office and serves faithfully.

She knows how to meet the public and spread "sunshine along life's pathway". Everyone who visits our church commends her for the way she keeps the church. She is well versed in the Scripture. A few weeks ago her mother visited her, she was overjoyed to find her daughter engaged daily in true Christian work in a noted church as "The Garden of Prayer" she wept for joy. She has five daughters and two sons.

Our little sister is a young woman, but she is anointed to pray each evening. She conducts the devotional services, the people are grateful for her and they assemble early to meet her in this great worship.

Chapter XV

Saved For The Purpose

"When Esther prayed and interceded for her people she humbled herself and addressed God before she contacted the King". Regardless of how people try to cast away the idea and thought of asking counsel from God for success I am a teacher of this. I am thankful for the pathway that leads to the mercy seat.

Dear reader it is interesting to know how we try to make ourselves known unto others by words and through the medium of prayer. Sometimes we fail utterly. I tried to present my prayer life unto others by telling them I as a "worm of the dust, a grain of sand, a door mat and many other insignificant objects". I thought this would present a beautiful picture of humility. This displeased the Lord, and He called me in question. I told Him I was trying to convey how completely surrendered my life was. He made me to know very definitely that He appreciated the idea of individuals representing themselves as children of the King. When I considered the matter I repented before Him; because He had washed me in His blood, and had given me a place in His divine inheritance.

I prayed that day, and the Lord asked me why I did not pray out into His glory. I told Him I was doing the best I could. I was willing to do more and go further if He would lead the way. He told me He had prayer plantations. Then I considered how many acres it required to make a plantation. I requested Him to give me a new acre in prayer. He asked me how often. I told Him momentarily. He led me on until I came to the place where I was able to inspire others to go forward and achieve new places in the prayer life with Him.

Many times letters come from young girls who are despondent and distressed. They request me to give them testimonies and instructions what they shall do when they finish college, and then, something occurs which prevents them from carrying out their plans. Before I close this book I shall tell you about a young woman who had similar experiences, and overcame each obstacle through prayer and consecration.

When the Lord sent Miss Ashley to assist me in the Letter Department, He also sent a very precious young lady, Miss Mary Passarella. The story of her life is outstanding and very interesting.

She received salvation when she was thirteen years old. Her friends tried to discourage her as friends will do. The told her she would never live for the Lord until she was twenty-one years old. She devoted her life to praying for the young children in the neighborhood and her family. Her desire was to win souls for Christ. She completed a course at the Eastern Bible Institute, at Philadelphia, Pennsylvania.

She was tested beyond measure, but the Lord opened the way whereby she graduated with honors. She was nineteen years old when she finished Bible School. She planned to travel and do the work of a praying evangelist. The devil knew the desires of this young soldier of the cross, therefore he touched her mother's body. She suffered excruciating pain and it wrecked her nerves. She was given the best medical care, but she did not respond, finally she had to be put in a sanatorium. There were four younger children to be cared for. Miss Passarella did not want to leave them in the street; hence she assumed the responsibility and cared for the family. She did not have anyone to encourage her, neither did she know anything about caring for the home.

She sought the Lord. He had compassion upon her, and taught her how to carry the responsibility which lasted for three years. She was Big Sister in this family circle, and because she gave herself to God, He supported her with His arms. She never purchased or decided anything for the family without consulting God first. As she fought victoriously the enemy tried to discourage her; because she was unable to achieve her intellectual ideals.

But the Word of the Lord taught her how to plead the blood against the contaminating, opposing powers of the devil. Two Scriptures were outstanding before her, "He that would live godly must suffer persecution" and "Cast your care upon the Lord for He careth for you", I love to hear her tell how she purposed in her heart never to displease, nor grieve her dear lovely Jesus. Sometimes her burdens were so heavy she buried her face in her hands, and wept before God, day and night, for Him to open a way and give her friends comfort and a place where she could work in His vineyard.

Temptations presented themselves greater, but the Lord watched over her and one day he led her to "The Garden of Prayer".

She completed a commercial course in high school, she was very efficient to help send the Word unto many hungry souls in all parts of the world from the Garden of Prayer. She realizes she was born for this work. Therefore she serves as unto the Lord, looking for the soon coming of her Lord on that Great Day; when the curtain shall be moved away, and she with the staff and many friends shall greet Jesus and rejoice for ever more. She is honest, trustworthy and a wonderful Bible teacher.

On Saturday evening our young people assemble to worship the Lord and deliver Bible messages. It is inspiring to see and hear these intelligent young people speak. Sinners are convinced and saved in these services. We call it the "Family Reunion Night".

CHAPTER XVI

His Prayer Life Influenced Me

Bishop Mason lives at Memphis, Tennessee. His work and humble devotion to Christ is noted throughout Christendom. I have told you how his conversation with God attracted my attention and stirred my enthusiasm to covet the spirit of prayer like unto his. He is a little man in stature, but his heart is big, and it is full of love and compassion for everybody everywhere.

He never converses with anyone early in the morning until after he has spent hours in prayer. The whole universe and its inhabitants are included in his prayers. His experienced, prayerful leadership and faith in God demonstrated in love for all humanity has put him in a class by himself.

I had the privilege of recording many of his prayers. I have witnessed how God answered him speedily. A few years ago there was a great drought in Lexington, Mississippi. Everything looked as though it was going to burn up for the lack of rain.

The people, the crops and the cattle were in grave danger. The Lord sent Bishop Mason home on Saturday. This was the time most farmers, and the people from the city, visited the little town. He was led to call a group of Christians together at nine o'clock that morning; and he prayed until four o'clock that afternoon. He never got up off his knees. While he groaned before the Lord beseeching Him to have mercy upon that place, and relieve that condition it began to thunder; and a few moments thereafter the rain fell.

He went to Durham, North Carolina, to visit Bishop Father's State Convention. Everything was suffering for the need of rain. He prayed; and that night the lord sent rain to the city. He had taught the people that day the Word of the Lord; recorded in second Chronicles the seventh chapter and the thirteenth and fourteenth verses. "If I shut up heaven that there be no rain, or if I command the locust to devour the land, or if I send pestilence among my people; if my people which are called by my name shall humble themselves and pray, and seek my face, and turn from their wicked ways, then will I hear from heaven, and will forgive their sins, and will heal their lane".

He left there and went to Pittsburgh, Pennsylvania to visit those dear faithful prayer warriors he loves so well. Enroute there the spirit of the Lord within him rebuked death. He was heavily burdened.

When he arrived in Pittsburgh it was so dry and hot he found the people sick and many had died from the heat. He fell on his face and prayed. The Lord answered him immediately. The rains fell and conditions changed.

The next day he went to Detroit, Michigan to meet the State's Convention. This was a serious time. At night it was so hot and dry the people left the buildings and went to the river to sleep. He was tired and worn in his body, therefore he sat by the wayside and taught the people of the Word of the Lord. He knelt and prayed. The Lord bound him there, and he groaned in the spirit; as if he was dying. Soon the clouds gathered together and formed a thick canvas in the sky. The people of God surrendered everything they had unto the Lord. It thundered as if it would shake the universe, and the lightening revealed itself.

Its flashes seemed to express gratitude unto the people that the Man of God's tears had been seen, and his prayer heard and answered. It began to rain. It seemed as if the flood gates had been opened. We had water everywhere. It filled the streets and the children on that old camp ground had to stand up on the seats to keep their feet from getting wet. Nobody had to make those people happy. They saw what prayer had done. It had covered the ground with water.

The revival broke out there was a day of thanksgiving and a time of jubilee. One day at Memphis, Tennessee during a large baptismal service he was preaching on the banks near the river. A great wind storm arose, the multitude did not know what to do, but he lifted up his hands and face heavenward, while he prayed the Lord gave peace and all was well.

This was such an amazing event the news reporters published articles and told the city how God worked for this man who prayed. Never shall I forget the time when a great tent meeting was in session in the city of Memphis.

Great preparation had been made in prayer for a soul saving revival. Bishop Mason was led to spend many hours in prayer on the ground. Suddenly a terrible storm arose; it seemed as if the hour of destruction had come. The spirit of the Lord lifted him off his knees and he cried unto the Lord to send peace and rebuke the storm. The Lord answered him immediately.

A very wicked man was in the service. When he beheld God's almighty handwork in that place he ran forward and fell at Bishop Mason's feet and cried, "It's enough," and the Lord saved his soul. The sick, sinners and backsliders made their way to that cleansing stream. The soul saving revival was great.

One evening Elder R.E. Heart announced his text under that same tent, it was, "Except ye abide in the ship you cannot be saved." Suddenly a wind storm struck that tent, and the tornado was traveling so fast it seemed as if everybody was going to be hurled into judgment. Bishop Mason fell on his face and prayed. He arose and rebuked the devil, and God answered his prayer.

After this, the revival fires broke out and the Lord confirmed His Word with signs. I am very thankful unto Him for this dear Prayer Warrior and strong minister, who has labored for over fifty years in the prayer ministry. Although he lives in the evening time of his life, I shall never forget the great love and fatherly care he has for me.

It was through the vision the Lord gave unto him and the General Supervisor Mother, Mrs. Lizzie Robinson, who lives in Omaha, Nebraska, I had the privilege to meet many of the noted leaders and serve in their churches. She and Bishop Mason have worked faithfully together for many years.

Chapter XVII

Healing Testimonies

PART I

Born With Heart Trouble

From the moment, I cried in the world I was afflicted. My mother did everything she could, but the doctor said I would be handicapped as long as I lived. I never knew what a well day was. I had to have treatments from doctors every two weeks. I took medicine until my system became immune, but it did not prevent me from having attacks. I had to stay in the bed two and three weeks at the time all of my life, sometimes longer.

I suffered this way for twenty-six years. On the 18th day of January, Nineteen hundred and forty-three, I had a heart attack which made me entirely helpless. I suffered as never before. My family rushed me to the hospital. I was treated and placed under the care of Dr. Griffith, one of Pennsylvania's best heart specialists. My condition became so acute he told my people it would carry me to my grave soon. They did not hide this from me. They wanted me to make my calling and election for heaven sure.

The time had come when I had to find the breast of Jesus. I knew it was only a matter of moments. I had heard of our Little Mother Dabney, how God had blessed her to pray for everybody, everywhere. I told my father and sister to go speedily and ask the woman of God to pray for me. She prayed for me, and on Monday morning about five o'clock I had a strange feeling, immediately a thought came into my mind, "The arms of the Lord".

When I considered this I felt that Jesus was there with me. The prayers from The Garden of Prayer had prevailed. About a week after they carried me home. I was not contented just to lie in bed as the doctors told me to do. I had faith in God, and in His people. I never doubted Him. I worried my family until they decided to carry me to The Garden of Prayer. They were dissatisfied because they thought it was to much for me; my husband took me in his arms like a baby and carried me into the church.

The first time I entered I was so sick I could not wait for Mother Dabney to pray for the sick.

They carried me home, I was miserable. I pleaded with them to carry me back; by this time I had really made up my mind what I wanted to do, and when our Little Mother prayed for me that night God gave me a new heart.

I walked that night. It was so wonderful I rejoiced, yea I rejoiced in the God of my salvation; as I had been unable to sit in a chair. I am stronger today, thank God for a place where we can go and God makes us whole in every detail. I work eight hours daily, six days weekly. The Lord not only healed my body, but He saved my soul and He saved my sister so that I would have somebody to go along with me in this great battle.

I shall ever render my service, faithfully in the church. Never shall I forget God and His precious Son Jesus.

This Scripture may encourage the hearts of those who have joined with us in this great universal prayer battle: "And it was so, that when Solomon had made an end of praying all this prayer and supplication unto the Lord, he arose from kneeling on his knees with his opened up to heaven. And he stood and blessed all the congregation of Israel with a loud voice saying, Blessed be the Lord, that hath given rest unto his people Israel, according to all that he promised, there hath not failed one word of all his good promise, which he promised by the hand of Moses his servant. The Lord our God be with us, as he was with our fathers: let him not leave us, nor forsake us: and his statutes and his judgments, which he commanded our father, and let these my words wherewith I have made supplication, before the Lord, be nigh unto the Lord our God day and night, that he maintain the cause of his servant, and the cause of his people Israel at all times, as the matter shall require. That all of the people of the earth may know that the Lord is God, and that there is none else. Let your heart, therefore be perfect with the Lord our God, to walk in his statutes and to keep his commandments, as at this day". I Kings 8:54-61.

Mrs. Cora Hinton,
1900-D No. 27th Street
Philadelphia, Pa.

HEALED OF BLEEDING ULCERS OF THE FEET

I was born in Virginia. Five years ago I was smitten with acute arthritis. For three years I could not walk at all. They operated upon me for broken veins, then I grew worse. For one year and eight months I was confined in the Philadelphia General Hospital. I had to be wheeled around in a chair. My condition was so acute the doctors did not have any hope for me and they told me to get all my business straight. They told me I would never be able to walk or work again. A friend told me to listen to the organ and the broadcast of the Garden of Prayer. It was so sweet I gained enough strength to be led to the church on two crutches.

That night I met Jesus. He broke my fetters and I walked all around the building. I left my crutches in the Garden of Prayer. Ever since then the Lord blessed me to work every day and care for myself. Thank God for a place like the church at 29th and Susquehanna Avenue.

Mrs. Henrietta Durnell,
2052 N. Warnock Street
Philadelphia, Pa

THEY LED ME TO THE GARDEN OF PRAYER

PART II

Dear   Friends:—

I was stricken on Wednesday the first day of September, Nineteen hundred and forty-three, with an acute appendicitis. My family physician rushed me to the hospital. Three doctors examined me. They decided I had to be operated on at once. They rolled me in a wheelchair to the operating room. They disrobed me and put me on the operating table. While they prepared the ether, the voice of God spoke to me saying, "What are you doing here? You do not need an operation." I knew who it was speaking to me, immediately I asked for privacy. I bent over and crept to the laboratory. I looked up to the ceiling and I prayed as never before. I really talked with my God, we were no strangers. I have known Him from a child. God did not wait until the cool of the evening, nor the early hours of the morning to come to me, but instantly He made it known unto me that He was with me and I could rely on Him.

I told Him I believed in His power to heal. I had preached it. I had encouraged others to trust Him; if He would give me strength I would refuse to be operated upon.

I went back to the room where the doctors were, and I told them my decision, they told me they were utterly surprised to hear a man as intelligent as I was talking as I was talking. But I stood upon my integrity; they told me if anything serious happened to me they would not be responsible. They made it very plain to me that my appendix would burst at any moment. They reminded me that it would cause death. This did not weaken my faith. I signed myself out the hospital, and called a cab and arrived home at two A.M., September the Second.

My precious wife is a noted school teacher and a real Christian. We prayed together until day. My misery was so intense it seemed almost impossible to go through. I called for a minister to pray for me, and anointed me with oil according to James fifth chapter, fourteen and sixteen verses. Somehow I held on to God, I knew I was in His hands to live or die. It was my desire that He should be glorified in my healing.

I believed in His divine Word which says, "All things are possible to him that believeth." My wife called the Garden of Prayer, and related the story to Sister Dabney. She requested her to come at once and pray for me, but she told her to give God the same privilege with me she had given the doctors. She requested her to bring me to church by nine o'clock sharp.

When I arrived there a minister was preaching; it seemed as if he never would stop. My left side was paralyzed, I was deathly sick. There was a host of sick people to be prayed for, and they left me for the last. The Lord was trying my faith and patience. Sister Dabney prayed for me, it was the sweetest prayer I ever heard, they laid hands on me, and God healed my body instantly.

I felt the hand of God when He operated upon me, nobody could make me doubt Him. I know when He completed the work. I went home and rested that night. The next morning, I looked after my business obligations.

Sunday I preached at my church, the Gospel Tabernacle Baptist Church, here in Philadelphia. Tuesday I boarded a crowded train and went to Chicago, Illinois, to our convention. The brethren were amazed; as they had received the message that it would be impossible for me to attend on account of serious illness. They wanted to know from me what had happened. I told them I was operated upon by the Master Surgeon Jesus the Son of God. I stayed there until the meeting closed. I boarded a crowded, congested train for Philadelphia; I had to stand nearly all the way home, but I felt fine. Today I am a well man and I never expect to die of appendicitis. Jesus fixed it for me, and it is all right. The time has come when we the ministers of the Lord must be living examples of God. He gives His ministers power to pray for the sick, and they are healed. I thank God for Elder Dabney and his praying wife. The sacrificial service they render in the Garden of Prayer is a God-sent blessing to this city and the world. It is a place where hospitality and Christian love never changes nor dies.

Rev. R. Howard Cook, A.M.; S.T.B.,
Philadelphia, Pennsylvania
Phone: Fremont 4906.

SUFFERED WITH HEART TROUBLE FIFTEEN YEARS

I was in critical condition, my heart was sick, I had the best of care from physicians, but nothing helped me. I fell and broke both of my arms. The heart attacks were so severe I had no control of myself. I went to the Doctors five and six times a day for needles to deaden the pain. I could not eat. I had to live on broth and other liquids. I was just a frame existing. Somebody told me a little lady was in town praying for everybody and God was working with her. I decided to go there. Someone carried me to the Garden of Prayer. The hallelujahs and glories were so sweet anybody would have been benefited. I was too sick to sit in the pew. Mother Dabney told me God did not have to patch my heart, He would give me a new one.

I was so frail, I did not think I could get down on my knees, but as she groaned my strength came and I knelt beside the altar. When she prayed I felt something break loose inside of me; immediately the Lord touched me and made me whole. He did not overlook my soul. He saved and healed me completely that night.

I went home that night a brand new woman. My husband and my child and my neighbors were amazed. The next day I went to my family physician for a checkup; after he examined me, he told me the last medicine he gave me cured my heart. He was delighted. I asked him was it really all right? He said, "yes, perfect." I told him it was not the medicine he gave me, I did not take it; he asked me what happened. I told him I found a little woman at the Garden of Prayer, and she told me that Jesus would give me a new heart. She prayed for me, I believed and Jesus healed me.

He became angry and declared he would put me out of his office if I continued that foolishness. He said it was terrible to have a woman in town like that. She would hinder all of his business. He asked me when was going to leave town. I told him never, she lives here. By this time his patients crowded around me to hear what Jesus had done through prayer. He ordered me out of his office.

I am yet healed. Since that time the Lord called that physician; and before he passed he and many of his friends called Mother Dabney in his behalf.

A few weeks ago I went to a noted Dentist here in Philadelphia to have my teeth extracted. I had to tell him how the Lord healed me of the heart trouble through prayer. He would not extract my teeth until I had received a thorough examination by the Doctors; this is the law for an individual who suffers or has suffered with heart trouble. I knew what the answer would be.

I work and care for my house each day. My heart never gets tired. I went to the doctor's and submitted to the examination. A few days ago the dentist received a letter from the doctor stating my heart is perfect.

Thank God for a praying woman in Philadelphia. If I was able I would fix it so that every sufferer would be brought to this Garden of Prayer. I trust my testimony will help and encourage some wayside sufferer. I sing in the choir, you know how much strength it requires to do this. I told the Lord I would lift up a standard for Him and use this heart he gave me. If the time comes when I need a new one I am going back to Jesus.

Mrs. Elsie Washington,
4093 Warren Street,
Philadelphia, Pa.

A TUMOR REMOVED FROM FACE

I had suffered for a long time. My eye sight was very bad. I had to wear glasses. I felt despondent. I did not want to go completely blind. I heard the Garden of Prayer and its kind, loving prayer warriors. I went there and our little sister prayed for me, the Lord restored my sight so perfectly I have not worn glasses since.

I suffered with an Asthmatic condition for twenty-five years. I suffered dreadfully with shortness of breath spells. If I walked or climbed steps it seemed as if it would be my last. For eight years I suffered intensely with a bad looking tumor on the side of my face, but when our little Mother Dabney prayed, immediately the tumor dissolved. I have never had any more trouble. Praise God from whom all blessings flow.

I decided to give the rest of my life praying for others. Many nights during the week and on weekends I spend my time praying in The Garden of Prayer. May God bless each one who reads this testimony. My face is perfect where the tumor was removed.

Mrs. Pauline Wimbley,
130 E. Stafford Street
Germantown, Philadelphia,
Pennsylvania.

A BLIND LADY RECEIVES HER SIGHT

Years ago I labored very hard to care for my family. I was very skillful with the needle, both sewing and crocheting. As I went on in life cataracts formed on both eyes. I went to many noted physicians, but they were unable to help me. Their only diagnosis was an operation. I knew I was too old for this, I was very despondent.

One night I heard our Little Mother Dabney pray over the Radio for everybody everywhere. I listened attentively as the announcer read excerpts from letters of people who had been healed while she prayed. I could not go anywhere alone. One night my daughter led me to The Garden of Prayer on Ridge Avenue. Mother prayed for me that night; immediately I began to see a little. I continued to go; eventually my daughter left the city and I had no one to carry me. I decided to test my eyes. I went by myself; this was encouraging to me and the people who had been accustomed to seeing me come in assisted. Then I began to sew. I made a dress for myself, and wore it to the Garden of Prayer. It looked so nice several of my friends had me to make dresses for them.

I did not have any trouble at all. I thread my machine and hand needles. I also had a dislocated spine for ten years. I was unable to get on my knees to pray; the doctors suggested an operation for this ailment also. I am seventy-two years old; therefore wisdom taught me my bones were too old to be operated upon. I trusted God. I was unable to walk a block without sitting on someone's steps to rest. While sitting in the meeting the Lord operated upon me. I went home healed. The next morning, I walked five blocks and did not stop to rest neither was I tired. While he was working on me He healed me of kidney trouble and rheumatism. I am healed to glorify God and praise His Name as long as I live.

Mrs. Jennie Howard,
3510 Mt. Vernon Street
Philadelphia, Pa.

PART III

HEALED FROM EATING CANCER

I suffered from a cancer or a number of years. I was in a horrible condition. I do not think any pain is any more excruciating than that caused by cancer. I was operated upon but it did not do me any good, I grew worse. The doctors did not hide from me the fact that I only had a few days to live. I did not pay any mind to what they said, still I knew I was dying on my feet. I did not doubt divine healing through prayer, but it was somewhat hard to find anyone who would take time to be concerned about a poor woman who was in my condition.

One night as I dialed my radio I heard the Garden of Prayer praying for everybody everywhere. Oh! I was so sick and weak I could hardly walk, but I pressed my way to the sweet place where Jesus was breaking the fetters and the bonds. I told God if He would heal me of that cancer I would go to the Garden of Prayer and stay there for the rest of my life. One Sunday night the glory of God was manifested in that place, the people were getting healed in a mighty way. I looked up and the Lord healed my body.

My dear friends, I have not been bothered with that cancer since. The doctor sent me a letter to come in for treatment. My heart leaped for joy. I had a grand chance to let him know how God healed me. I told him I did not need another doctor. Jesus paid it all for me. Thank

God for the Garden of Prayer and people who have unlimited faith with the Lord in this very dark day.

Mrs. Lela Bolling,
766 N. Lex Street,
Philadelphia, Pa.

STUDENT NURSE HEALED

I was in training, while in school I had a nervous breakdown, and I had to discontinue my training. I was sick for three years under the care of some of the best physicians, but my case baffled them. They made X-ray pictures of my stomach and my chest at the Jefferson Hospital, 10th and Sansom Streets, Philadelphia, Pennsylvania. After the Doctors held a consultation together they told me to go home and stay in bed. I found out that they thought by this time I would be dead, but I heard of the Garden of Prayer. My sister carried me there. When Mother Dabney prayed the power of God overshadowed my body and I fell out.

I was in a coma all night. My brother came to the church and took me home. I was in a beautiful place where the flowers were blooming, the grass was green and there was a lovely white background. I stood and listened to the singing like the sweet voices of angels. That choir seemed to have been far away. I could feel the power penetrating through me. I felt better than I ever felt in my life. My sister thought I was dead, but the Lord was only working with me.

When I reacted all of my distress was in my throat; I told my family I wanted to vomit; after this was over I was completely well. I was so happy and light I felt like I could fly somewhere. I only weighed 107 ¼ pounds. I thank God for His divine touch, now I weigh 121 pounds.

The Lord not only healed me, but He saved my soul. I can eat whatever I desire. My testimony has been a great help to many individuals, even my dear, loving father, who passed a few months ago. Not only was he touched in his body, but he caught faith and the Lord blessed his soul a few moments before he passed. He requested me to convey to Mother Dabney and the church his greetings, and let them know he was going to be with Jesus, I tell it wherever I go. I am not saying this to honor Mother Dabney, she would not accept this, but I give God the glory and thanksgiving, for letting a woman like her live in a time like this. One who knows how to pray through, and has the spiritual ability to teach others how to do likewise. May God bless each one who reads my testimony.

Mrs. Lessie Seagraves,
4628 Brown Street,
Philadelphia, Pa.

Dedicated to the Garden of Prayer Bible Band and Missionaries

One night I had a vision,
Kneeling by my bedside in prayer.
I saw the Garden, and its mission.
And you were working there.
I saw the people pressing,
I heard the tramp of their feet.
They came to receive a blessing.
Their faces were tender and sweet.
I saw the great altar where souls
Had gathered for the hour of prayer.
Beneath the altar were live coals.
The glory of God was there.
They brought the sick and afflicted.
All nations were anxious to share.
Sinners, both men and women were convicted,
As the spirit led out in prayer.
I observed when this service ended,
Jesus was not in the Garden alone.
They marched forward and gave an offering.
(While the organ played, "The Fight Is On.")
I beheld the great communion services.

You were dressed in spotless white.
You did not seem to be nervous.
Co-workers, this was a glorious night.
I saw the people standing,
When the benediction prayer was prayed.
They passed out without entertaining.
Like soldiers in an army array.

PRAYER

Send the former and the latter rain, O my God.
Send the refreshing showers again.
Send help to those at home and abroad.
Give us godly patience to stand.
Our mothers and fathers are crying for meat.
The youth are deep in despair.
The nations can scarcely find enough to eat.
Forgive, dear God, and answer my prayer.
This generation ignored your great command.
It has brought darkness, famine, and death.
Sometimes it's so cold we cannot stand.
Then it's so warm we can hardly draw our breath.
Please close this war which is very mean.
Teach us how to live together again.
You are the greatest general, you are the greatest dean.
Forgive and blot out our sins.
Smile on the soil, touch it with your blood.
In Jesus' name I pray.
Rebuke the storms, and turn away the floods,
That will carry our products away.
Our God when you send rain upon the earth,
Give it healing balm to cure.
Unstop the blood streams, add forgiving myrrh.
Deliver your own once more.
Turn away your anger Lord, and smile.
Let nation repent, love, sow and reap.
The greater day shall come with trials.
I pray Thee our souls do keep.

Amen.

Dedicated to Miss Christine Jones

My friend and I always agree
In counsel precious and true.
Sometimes, it's so dark I cannot see.
He whispers let me walk with you.
When the evening calls the roll for those
Who have toiled to go to sleep,
I bid good-bye to life's cares and foes.
Then over the rocks we leap.
Just to know He came for me,
Sends tears coasting down my cheeks.
When I think how His blood has made me free,
I leap for another prayer mountain peak.
I converse with Him all night long.
I ask blessings for everybody everywhere.
Then my soul greets Him in songs.
Thank you for the fellowship we share.
He sends the rain upon my soul,
He filled my heart with right.
He blesses my body with health like gold.
Come, "dear ones", and join me in this flight.
When the morning birds come out and sing,
When voices are heard in the streets,
The prayer bells in my soul begin to ring.
Thank you God, our visit was complete.
Fight on, my soul, fast and pray.
Do not murmur by the way.
The gates of gold will not close,
Until He leads us there to stay.
At the table on that precious day,
I shall enjoy a feast once more.
The cries of the needy will pass away,
When we gather there to work no more.

PART V

A BROKEN BODY MADE WHOLE

Two years ago I heard the Garden of Prayer over the air. The music, the songs and the Word arrested my attention. I went to the Garden of Prayer, and as the Lord wonderful story and her testimony how God blessed her to pray through.

I had suffered many ailments and afflictions for eighteen years. My body was weak and my mind was mentally ill. My friends and family looked forward to the time when I would be put in an institution for nervous disorders. After listening to the little mother's testimony I decided there was hope for me. That night the Lord broke my bonds and fetters and delivered me. Not only did the Lord touch me but He touched my child, she will soon be nineteen years old. The doctors say she has a mentality of a child four years. I gave Mother Dabney the request, God answered her prayer and this answer has amazed my family and friends. Today my daughter is operating a power machine.

I was a diabetic. I suffered everything that accompanies that disease. Today I am enjoying better health than I have for many years.

Since the Lord has blessed me I have given up all to follow, to work and to help build up the kingdom. My greatest ambition is to become a prayer warrior. It is my desire to pray for people everywhere, and have that favor with God that when I pray He will answer and the people will be benefited. I used to wear glasses, the Lord has given me youthful sight; therefore I have discarded them. May God bless the Garden of Prayer and each one who reads this testimony.

Mrs. Laurella Dorsey,
935 N. 65th Street
Philadelphia, Pa

Dedicated to Rev. and Mrs. Charles E. Robinson,
Springfield, Mo.

There is a place where the sick can go
When they are feeble, weak and sad.
Our Garden of Prayer is an open door,
Like Paul and Peter Had.
There is a group with hearts that pray,
They try to do their best.
Their hands are outstretched night and day,
To help some poor soul find rest.
There is a groan that never fails,
Regardless how dark your way.
Thank God for Christians who really care
For everybody everywhere today.
Just a few miles up the road, where you thought
You will meet our Shepherd there;
He will know you by the word you taught
Each day when you lived here.
No more waiting for the "Turnkey" to open the door
Where you delivered His Word to those in the cell.
You shall rest from the cares of this world and its woes
When the smiles on His face shall tell you it is well.

SAVED FROM THE WRECK

For seventeen years I suffered with sleeping sickness. I had no control of myself whatsoever. I would fall asleep while standing up washing dishes. Many times while standing at the ironing board I would fall asleep and the iron would get red hot and burn through the garment, the pad and the board. I would go to the door to bid friends good-bye and would fall asleep before I closed the door. I would go in the telephone booth, drop my nickel and before the operator could get the number I was sleep.

The people pitied me and gave me work. Many times while I was up on the ladder washing windows I would fall asleep. The madam would have to come and awaken me. I made money but went to sleep on the trolley and lost it or someone took it from me. I was in a terrible condition. One night I heard Mother Dabney pray on the Radio. I wrote her a letter, she answered me and sent a blessed handkerchief, her letter was so sweet I decided to go to church. The Lord completely healed me. I work in a hospital all day; I never get sleepy. Many times I spend my weekends in the Garden of Prayer with Jesus.

I pray all night long the Lord saved me from the wreck, and gave me perfect health to serve Him. I work faithfully in the church. I sing in the choir. Thank God for our Little Mother whom God is using to help the poor distressed people find the way to the mercy seat of the Lord.

Mrs. Willamenia Campbell,
Philadelphia, Pa.

PART V

HE DID THE IMPOSSIBLE

I was very comfortable with my dear husband and home life. The enemy afflicted my body; I suffered day and night with heart trouble. I became so serious and helpless they put me in the Pennsylvania Hospital. I remained there for six weeks, I was nothing better, but I grew worse. I had care from the best doctors but it puzzled them and they finally admitted that they could do nothing for me.

They advised my family to put me in a Convalescent Home. My husband was so deeply concerned about my condition he agreed. Finally they gave me three weeks to live. But God did not want me to go to sleep; He permitted me to go back to my home. My dear little niece told me about the Garden of Prayer. They carried me there. The presence of God was very great. Elder Dabney was greatly anointed to preach the Word of God. He talked about Faith. He told us about a man who waited all night in Los Angeles, California prayer meeting when Mother Dabney prayed there. He related the story how they had to lead that man to the building. The next morning the glory of God fell from heaven. That poor, sick man opened his coat and cried, "Jesus, don't pass me by."

When I heard about the great faith of this man the hands of my soul reached out and touched Him. Immediately the Lord healed me. This was Sunday night.

Monday morning I arose early and washed a three weeks' wash. I have been working three days a week ever since.

I suffered with acid in my blood. It gave me discomfort and pain. I went to the doctor for information. He prescribed a diet. I would have to take needles frequently. I testified one night that I was tormented with this affliction. The Lord, through our Little Sister, reminded me how He had delivered me of a sick heart two and a half years ago. Immediately I repented in my heart, thanksgiving broke out in my soul. Thank God He healed my body.

Not only did the Lord render this kind favor unto me, but He healed my husband also. Nobody will ever have any trouble with me. I shall give God the glory. I am confident of this one thing, I know it is impossible for man to give you a new heart. This one the Lord gave me that night seems to be made out of better material than the one I was born with. I am absolutely enjoying life as never before. Whatever affliction you suffer carry it to my Jesus in prayer. He will fix it for you.

Mrs. Eva Costin,
429 South 8th Street,
Philadelphia, Pa.

PRAYER PREVENTED ME FROM GOING
TO AN ASYLUM

I married when I was young. My father was a carpenter by trade, my mother was an ideal Christian. I had nothing to hinder me from making life worthwhile if I had taken my proper rest. I had great ambition. The Lord gave me seven children. I over worked myself. I had a nervous breakdown, my mind left me, I was helpless.

It grieved my dear wife and mother, but the time had come when they had to seek protection for the family and for me likewise. The doctors made preparation to put me in Byberry Asylum. Above all, I was soul sick; a man with a large family and a lost soul. I did not know anything about God and His Son, Jesus. I did not have mind to understand what my mother and friends tried to tell me about Him. I had to work young, I knew almost nothing about the Sunday School and church. One day Mother Howard, the lady who received her eyesight in The Garden of Prayer, visited our home. It was only God who made me tell her I would permit her to carry me to the place where devils was subject and cast out in the Name of Jesus.

When I entered the church I was too mentally deranged to pay any attention to what anybody said. I just looked around, I felt funny and strange. Mother and Elder Dabney were praying so sincerely for everybody. When I knew anything I was clothed in my right mind. I had the experience for the first time of witnessing even my own self to be a human man again.

The first thought came to me was, Praise the Lord, the Lord saved me, thank God. I work every day and make a comfortable living for my family. The Lord gave me back to my wife, our dear little children and my sweet mother. I felt like going everywhere and gathering up the sick and afflicted in mind and bring them here to this place where Jesus restored my mind.

M.H. Harvey,
3835 Melon Street,
Philadelphia, Pa.

HEALED FROM AN ACCIDENT IN AN AUTOMOBILE

One night enroute home from church service a car collided with ours, and turned it over. It knocked me unconscious; they rushed me to the hospital, the doctors thought I would have lost my eyesight. I was in a frightful condition. It did not seem possible I should live to tell the story. My husband carried me home, and called for our pastor, Elder Dabney. When he arrived he prayed for me; the soreness left and the Lord healed me without leaving a scar.

When I accepted salvation my husband was very sick. We tried everything to assist him; but everything failed. I joined the Garden of Prayer when Mother Dabney and our pastor entered their second mission on Sharswood Street. Of course, he did not believe so much in trusting the Lord to heal through prayer; therefore it was very hard for me to encourage him to permit the people of God to pray for his deliverance.

His friends weakened his faith with unfriendly conversations. He made up his mind to give up the ghost and die. I had to work each day to help support the home, sometimes all night I had to toil with him.

One day he decided to let our Mother and Pastor pray for him. His eyes had sunk deep, his skin looked like it was covered with syrup. He was just a skeleton. When they prayed for him they asked the Lord to heal his body if he would get saved and work in the church lifting up a standard for Jesus.

That night he promised the Lord he would walk with Him if He healed his body. When our leaders prayed, God delivered my husband from the stocks of death. He saved his soul; I am happy to say he is one of the honored deacons of the Church. My own mother stood faithfully by my side until this day. I trust each one who reads my testimony will receive inspiration and encouragement. If your family is afflicted and burdened write in to the Garden of Prayer.

One thing I admire they never cast you aside or get tired of praying for those who are in need.

Mrs. Nannie Powell,
4510 Wyalusing Avenue,
Philadelphia, Pa.

THE WANDERER MET THE WONDERFUL JESUS

I was absolutely crazy, I had lost my mind, I had become so serious preparations had been made to put me in an institution. I boarded street cars, buses, elevated trains and rode all day. I did not have sense enough to get off. I did not know what I wanted or where I was going. I did not know Jesus.

One night I was out wandering, I wandered to North Philadelphia. Something like a strong wind took hold of my skirt and pulled me into the Garden of Prayer where Mother Dabney was praying.

She was very kind and sweet looking to me. I admired her, but I did not have sense enough to tell her my name. In other words, I did not know it. My whole body was covered with lumps and knots. I did not have sense enough to go to a doctor to get help. Now I thank God that I did not go. Mother Dabney called me to the altar. I had forgotten how to walk, but that same thing that pulled me into the church led me to the altar. When Mother Dabney prayed and groaned in the spirit she wept as if her heart would break before the Lord for my deliverance; immediately I came to myself. I could hear those groans and words she uttered in prayer. She rebuked the devil. The Lord broke my fetters and bonds, opened the prison door and turned my soul unto Him.

I lifted up my head, for the first time I called Jesus, He washed me in His blood that night and gave me a clean mind and a pure, praying mind. I am able to work and make a living. I am an usher in the Garden of Prayer, the Lord blesses me to usher the large crowds that come to this place continually. My mind has never been disturbed since.

Miss Mary Berkeley,
4232 Fairmount Avenue,
Philadelphia, Pa.

HEALED OF INFLUENZA

I was smitten with influenza. I had suffered with heart trouble for many years. This made me very weak. The physicians were unable to help me. I made up my mind to give up the ghost, and let the Lord carry me to rest. My husband called my Pastor and Mother to pray for me. When they arrived I knew the Lord was with them, but I did not want to live. I tried to get my husband to stop praying for the Lord to heal my body, but he is such a dear companion and Christian man he held on.

When death struck me I knew it; my Leaders also knew it. Miss Ashley and my friend, Mrs. Phillips, were in the room. My Pastor groaned in the spirit; he and Mother Dabney rebuked death from my body and the Lord made me whole. A few nights thereafter the same affliction seized my husband's body. I did not have a phone to call my pastor: I prayed and rebuked the devil, and God delivered him. The Lord blessed me to play the piano. I told Him if He would heal my husband's body and give him strength to work in the church I would give Him my hands as long as I live. The Lord is a healer. I trust my testimony may inspire some wife and husband who may have a similar experience.

Mrs. Lillian Robinson,
1714 N. 18th Street,
Philadelphia, Penna.

HEALED OF DEAFNESS

When I arrived in Philadelphia from Norfolk, Virginia, I went to the mission where Mother and Elder Dabney prayed both day and night. It was my heart's desire to learn how to contact God and pray. I was deaf, I suffered with a roaring in my head, it was serious. I went to church one night. I wept because I could not enjoy the services. The minister preached, but I was just there. I knew the Lord was dear in my soul, fully able to help me. I did not exercise faith, I returned home despondent and distressed.

One evening I went to the mission early; prayer ascended for the sick. I suffered excruciating pains in my eyes and head. The Lord did not pass me by; He touched my body and healed me instantly. Then I was touched with the way Mother Dabney prayed. She did not mind fasting and praying; what the people said did not decrease her love for Jesus. Therefore she gathered us around her as a real mother and taught us how to press by everything to achieve a place with the Lord. I watched her. I saw this house in its first and second glory. I am well pleased with the leaders He gave me. I have found out what David means when he said, he desired to dwell in the house of the Lord all the day of his life.

They have made "Christian living" such a reality in our lives, I am enthused and thankful the Lord led me to this place.

Deafness is a horrible affliction. I could not keep a position as I could not hear. Many times people suffer with the same affliction for years, because no one ever takes time to pray for their healing. The Scripture said, if any are afflicted let him pray. If you will do this your healing will come, if it is the will of God. I trust each one who reads my testimony may be inspired to look up and accept your blessing.

Mrs. Flora King
2041 College Avenue,
Philadelphia, Pennsylvania

BLIND AND HELPLESS

"The Lord is night unto them that call upon Him, to all that call upon Him in truth".

Dear Reader:—

No matter what way we turn, we are sure to meet with the power and presence of Him. Darkness may surround you; friends may be far from you; earth, death and hell may level their poisonous darts at the children of God; but no matter what occurs you are protected when the Lord is with you. All you have to do is retain His divine favor is to keep your character and heart pure. You will claim the promise and the victory. I tried Him when I was helpless and proved Him when I was in despair.

Almost a year ago I was afflicted. I could neither walk nor see. I had become helpless, they had to feed me like a little baby. I heard about the little praying woman at the Garden of Prayer who prays for everybody everywhere. The Lord put it upon the heart of a friend of mind to hire a taxi cab and carry me to the Garden of Prayer. Three ushers with my friend and the cab driver assisted me into the building. I was too weak to hold up my head. Mother Dabney prayed for me. I felt the hand of God when it touched me that night my eyes came open, I started to walk, but my ankles were weak.

When I went home they wanted to assist me out of the taxi, but I told them I was healed. I went into the house, my husband was going to help me up the steps, but I told him to follow me.

And God let me go to my bedroom alone. It was on the twenty-ninth day of November, Nineteen hundred and forty-three, When God healed me. I have not suffered with that affliction since. I can see, I walk, I go anywhere I want to.

Dear friends, let me tell you it is a wonderful thing to have a place like The Garden of Prayer on the earth today. Many people call it The Prayer Garden Spot of the World. A few days ago I went to the seashore to visit my friends. They were amazed to see me healed and blessed. Not only has the Lord blessed my body but my soul. I am ready to work in His house. I am sending you my testimony praying it will help many of you who are in bondage and afflicted. It is nothing strange for the blind to receive their sight in this place. Not only are the sick bodies healed but the dark hearts are enlightened and their sinful souls are washed in His blood. The believers are sealed with His Holy Spirit according as he said it would be.

Mrs. Tyler
Philadelphia, Pennsylvania

HEALED OF CANCER OF THE THROAT

One day I heard of Mother Dabney and the Garden of Prayer. How the sick were healed, blind receiving their sight; the lame were leaping with joy; cancers and tumors were removed, and all manner of diseases were healed.

I received a call from friends in Detroit, Michigan, stating that my brother was in the hospital suffering with a cancer of the throat, and besides had lost his mind. He was so bad that they had strapped him to the bed.

I had my daughter to call Mother Dabney immediately, and asked her to pray for him. She did and the Lord marvelously worked in his behalf. When I walked in the hospital the next day he was sitting up in bed clothed and in his right mind.

I talked with the doctors, they were amazed. They could not understand what had happened. The change was instantaneous and they were baffled. I know that my God will baffle the most learned. The next day I went to the hospital again. I met my brother walking around and perfectly sane.

I shall never forget Him for His great kindness unto us in this time of trouble. I thank you for holding on in prayer for us, I am sure if you had not petitioned God in his behalf, he would have been gone. I am returning to Philadelphia the last of this week and I shall see you. Pray on, Mother Dabney.

Mrs. Leila Hatcher
2214 N. 21st Street
Philadelphia,Pennsylvania

When my son joined the U.S. Army Service the Lord sent a sixteen year old boy to announce for our Radio Broadcast. He sent me little Horace Sheppard.

He was converted when he was very young. He has a dear mother and sister. Little Horace is the bread winner in that home. It is very unusual to see a boy assume the responsibility of home life. Because of conditions he had to attend night school. He has been my announcer for two years; this has made a great difference in his life, experience is our best teacher. Mr. Sheppard is now a young man full of ambition and a desire to do something for God and for fallen humanity everywhere.

The Lord has called him to preach and it is my desire to have him continue his education.

Each Sunday evening our Radio audience is greatly impressed by the intelligent way in which he reads the excerpts from letters received from all parts of the world. The Lord has blessed this ministry through him.

EXCERPTS FROM FOREIGN FIELD LETTERS

South Nigeria, West Coast Africa

Dear Sister:

Thank God for your prayer life. We have been greatly inspired here by reading your article, "What It Means to Pray Through", published in one of our Christian magazines. May God bless you.

U.A. Ekanem. Esqr.

Brown's Town, Jamaica,
British West Indies

Dear Sister and Mother:

Thank you for your kind letters and prayers. Through friends I learned of your wonderful work. They sent me several magazines which published articles concerning your daily walk with God in prayer. We are praying with you.

Yours in His Service,
C.C.H.

Wrangell, Alaska

Dear Little Sister:—

I am impressed with your prayer life. I need God to heal my body. I shall pray with you as much as I can.

Yours in Him,

Old Hill Staff, England.

Dear Sister in the Lord:—

I rejoice in the blood of Jesus. Very happy to hear how He has put you in His "Prayer Bonds". May He strengthen you as we need this type of ministry.

Your fellow servant,
A.H.B.

Co. Tyrone, North Ireland

Dear Sister:—

Greetings, I have heard how the Lord has anointed you to pray continually. This good news certainly encourages my heart. Remember me, nothing is too hard for God.

Yours sincerely in Jesus,
Miss M.F.

———————

Valparaiso, Chile, South America

Dear Co-Worker:—

I enjoy your personal letters. Prayer is the need of the hour. Thank God for the way He has placed me on your heart. Yes, I shall pray with you.

Yours for Calvary's sake,
L.M.H.

———————

Shikee, Yunnan Prov., Southwest China.

Dear Sister:—

I know you will be surprised to receive a letter from this remote corner of the earth. I read an article how God has blessed your humble life. It was so precious and encouraging. I am forwarding this air-mail letter to you to let you know I shall be praying with you. Please write at once.

Yours Looking for that blessed Hope,
A.E.R.

Nadakavu St. Mavaelikara P.O. Travancore, India.

Beloved in Christ:—

Your call to prayer letter stirred my soul; as I am a prayer warrior also. It certainly made m soul happy when I read your letter and the Word of God. I know you have a great responsibility, dear sister, but your reward shall be great also. I shall pray with you.

Yours for the soon coming of our Lord,
J.C.E.

———

Castanduva, Est., de sao. Paulo Brazil

Dear Sister:—

Your address was forwarded to me by a friend. Also the booklet telling of God's leading in your life of prayer has been sent to me in Spanish and English. It is a soul stirring message. May God bless you to press onward this news is very sweet and precious to us. We shall pray for you and with you. Do not forget us.

Yours in His love,
M.L.B. deG.

Poste Restante Djambia, Sumatra Northeast India

Dear Little Sister:—

I enjoyed reading your interesting letter. May God bless you and your ministry of prayer. We shall be praying with you at this end of the line.

His and Yours in prayer
Rev. H. M.

Malaga, Santander, Columbia, South America.

Dear Prayer Warrior:—

We enjoyed your lovely call to prayer letters. They are filled with the Lord's wholesome words. Yes, we shall pray with you. We have to work hard here but we know the secret of our success comes through constant prayer. May the Lord strengthen and protect your health. We have been through great tests, but prayer has changed things.

Yours faithfully in His service,
Elder and Mrs. B.B. and Family

Nigeria, West Africa

Dear Sister Dabney:—

We have been informed by our pastor here that you stand before the Lord in prayer continuously for the sick in soul and body everywhere. Please pray for me and all of my people. I have a great desire in my heart to do something for God while I am young. I need my body healed. Please write.

Yours in Christ,
M.F.

Allahabad U.P. India.

Dear Beloved:—

Thanks for your prayers, we feel the effects here. It will be marvelous if God will lead you here to pray in this place some day. We are holding on to God with you. Write often: your letters are so inspiring it encourages us to read them to our people.

Yours in Christ,
F.A.G.

Via Ikot Ekpene, North Coast Africa.

Dear Sister in Christ:—

Many of our people have been healed through your prayers and blessed handkerchiefs. I am a minister, please ask your Father God to let you come here and pray some day. We love to hear the missionaries talk about how God uses you. I love God with all my heart; I want to be a soul winner.

Yours in His service,
Y.M.A.U

Orange Free State, South Africa

Dear Little Sister:—

Your letters are so full of the good Gospel, our hearts are happy over here. Many people have been healed by applying the blessed handkerchiefs you sent. I am a child of God. When I read your letters I feel the power of God all over me. I pray He will give you strength and encourage you never to let go. An article published in one of our magazines told us how you love everybody everywhere. May God bless your ministry to cover the earth.

I would like to receive all I can in this country to help my people. I trust someday may rise in your country to help me to go to school there. I will stay at the altar continually. I will meet you at the Throne of God.

Your brother in Christ,
B.E.B

Wentworth Park, Grugersdorf, South Africa.

Dear Sister Dabney:—

Your letter arrived in time with blessed handkerchiefs to help many of the people and children who were sick with tropical fever. We know God doeth all things well, and it is God in you that gives you love and power to pray today. Dear Sister, we cut your letters and envelopes in squares and applied them to the bodies of the sick—God blessed in a great way. Keep on praying, you may be sure praying Africa will meet the praying Garden of prayer there in America somewhere before the Throne of God continually.

Yours longing for His coming,
C.M.

New Mexico, D.F.

Dear Sister:—

Your tract stirred my heart. I observed you are calling all Christian women to prayer. I was very sick in January with terrific pains and fever. The Lord healed. I am a firm believer in prayer. I shall tell my friends to join with you in prayer.

Your Sister in Christ,
A.S.

Capetown, South Africa

Dear Little Sister:—

I hope and trust God that this letter reaches you. I have read articles published in our noted Christian papers and magazines how God blesses you to pray always. Oh! Sister it stirred my heart; it has been a long time since I heard of anyone living humble enough to walk with God as you do. I feel that longing in my soul to go further with Him. Surely if He blessed you He has other blessings waiting for those who will suffer and pay the price as you did. I want to meet you. In Jesus' Name.

Yours in Christ,
E.T.

Buenos Aires Argentina Republic

Dear Sister:—

We carried your tract from door to door and the Christian people rejoice to know you have contacted our God. Please send us more information concerning your prayer life. It must be wonderful to have such faith and favor today in the Maker of all things.

Yours in Christ,
A.N. de An.

New Zealand

Dear Sister Dabney:—

It is a glorious privilege to know a dear, humble child of God like you in these dark hours of distress and sorrow. Your letters are strength and wisdom. I am sending you a long list of Names of prayer warriors who have joined with you in this great prayer battle. Please write often.

Yours in Christ,
A.S.

———⋙⋅⋘———

Springdale Hall, Bay Newfoundland

Dear Sister in Christ:—

Please ask God to heal my body. I know if He will hear anybody He will hear your prayer. I felt the power all over me as I read an article of how God has blessed you. It is wonderful to go out into His holy mountain and stay there until He presents you unto His children. I shall be delighted to see your crown in heaven.

Yours in Christ,
F.H.

Wellawatte Colombo, Ceylon and India.

Dear Sister:—

You do not know me, but I read an article concerning your devotion and prayer life. It is so precious to know you have obligated yourself to pray for everybody; while you pray, please remember our six children in England.

Yours in His service,
Mr. and Mrs. V.C.

———⋙⋅⋘———

Shanghai.

Little Sister:—

The precious story about your humble prayer life refreshed my soul. I am confident if you continue this sacrificial life of suffering and prayer for everybody the cold, stony hearts of nations will soon be broken everywhere.

Yours in His Bonds,
E.A.

District Thana, Fort Bombay, India.

Dear Sister Dabney:—

We are saved under His precious blood. Thank you for your lovely letters and pamphlets, they inspire our souls. Yes we are praying with you and for you. May God strengthen you.

Yours for the salvation of souls,
B.B.B.

Hong Kong Colony.

Little Sister of Prayer:—

I think your letters are timely, we shall join you in prayer. I do not know how long we shall work here; wherever we go our souls shall pray with you.

M.B.B.

Dondaiche, W. Khandesh, India.

Dear Sister:—

Thanks for your lovely call to prayer letters and tracts. Pray for souls to be saved in this place, please. I was despondent, but your letter inspired and lifted me. I love to read. I shall meet you at the mercy seat continually in prayer.

O.J.

Mogok, Burma.

Dear Sister:—

Through one of our noted religious magazines I read about your prayer ministry. This encouraged me so much I must write and acknowledge the same to you. I think it is marvelous how you have humbled yourself to pray for everybody everywhere. Oh, dear sister, we need this type of ministry. I shall pray with you as I am a prayer warrior also.

Yours in His service,

Transvaal, South Africa.

Little Sister:—

There is joy and comfort in your letters. My dear wife and I have been greatly inspired how God has led you into the realms of prayer. Enclosed you will find a large number of names of some of our noted leaders here who will meet you somewhere around the throne of God.

Yours in His love,
Rev. J.M.M.

Beirut, Lebanon, Syria.

Beloved Little Sister:—

Your inspiring letters received. May God bless your great work. We have many faithful prayer warriors here who are praying for God to break through. We shall pray for you.

Yours for His service,
R.R.

Callao, Peru.

Dear Sister Dabney:—

Articles published about your prayer ministry made my heart rejoice. Thank God He has found someone to stand in the Gap. Eze. 22:30.

Yours in Christ,
Mrs. P.H.H.

Vancouver, British Columbia, Canada.

Little Sister in Christ:—

In days like these good news comes only seldom. I received a letter from you today. I leaped for joy, it is the sweetest letter I have read for ages. This must be the turning point. Many of the precious, faithful children of God have wailed day and night for God to raise up somebody who will pray as the men of old and the women likewise. I trust you will come to Canada. A warm, Christian welcome awaits you. You said you plan to go to England some day, please make your first visit here. May God bless you.

Your sister in Christ,
E.E

Ottawa, Ontario, Canada.

Beloved:—

May the glory of God overshadow you. I write to let you know the Lord healed a brother who was given up to die a few days ago. After you prayed for him he revived. He requested me to write you how wonderfully God answered your intercessory prayer.

Yours in Christ,
M.A.

Peterborough, Ontario, Canada.

Little Sister:—

Your letter received and the handkerchiefs, thank you in the Name of Jesus. I placed one of my face, my husband was not saved and he objected. I told the Lord to work in His own way and remove the growth from my face. A few mornings passed, I went to the mirror to wash my face with my wash cloth, and the Lord touched that growth, it disappeared. My husband and I went to breakfast, I did not tell him the growth had disappeared, when he saw it had gone he ran to me with outstretched arms and repented for all his misdeeds. He wanted me to call you by long distance. I know you are a very busy woman, but for his sake I tried to contact you. Your lines were busy continually. I am sending you this letter to let you know our God is a wonder in prayer.

Yours for His service,
A.R.

Port Alberin, British Columbia, Canada.

Sister Dabney:—

Your lovely letter received. I am sending it to a friend in England. Our mother has been ill for years. Through your prayers God touched her body. She is able to care for herself again. Darling, little child of God, keep praying, your ministry is in great demand today. I think it would be wonderful if you could send your letters all over the world.

Your sister in Christ,
S.A.

———

Montreal, Canada.

Dear Sister Dabney:—

The article published concerning the experience you received through suffering in your church continually has stirred my soul. That article has been a great blessing to many of my friends also. I know you are a child of God. It is somewhat hard to believe anyone lives today like you. However, the magazine that carried your article publishes the truth only. I trust you will write me. I think it will be a wonderful thing to receive a letter from a woman of God like you.

Yours in Christ,
H.L.

Tisdale, Saskatchewan, Canada.

Dear Sister Dabney:—

A few days ago friends and I conversed together with a desire in our hearts to contact somebody who had a real experience of walking with God as the prayer warriors of old, Martin Luther, Wesley and others. This morning the mailman delivered a magazine with an article concerning you. We feel this letter was an answer to prayer of real hearted women and men. We shall find out more about you in the near future. Some of our people are coming there to visit you.

Yours in Christ,
S.Y.

———————

Winnipeg, Man., Canada.

Dear Sister:—

I have been so blessed by the Holy Spirit which overshadowed your letters. I feel like a new woman. Thank God for the way He uses you. My two daughters have been saved since you last heard from me. Thank God for your sweet prayers.

I suffered with a rupture; it gave me much trouble, thank God I am healed. When I read the testimony of the lady who received her sight in your Garden of Prayer I held on to faith. It is wonderful what God can do through letter writing. May God bless you.

Your sister in Christ,
U.L.

———————

Saskatoon, Sask., Canada.

Dear Sister:—

I read about your wonderful experience in an article. It filled my heart with joy to know God has raised you up to pray in this evil day. My soul shall pray with you for everybody everywhere. You said the Lord will send the rain. I believe this with all my heart.

Yours in Jesus' Name,
H.T.

Indianhead, Sask., Canada.

Dear Sister Dabney:—

The article published in the *Pentecostal Evangel* stirred my soul. I have been a worker in the Lord's vineyard for a long time. But in the last few years revivals have not been what they used to be; therefore, I felt discouraged. I wept bitterly when I read the article about you. I know if God has blessed you, which I am confident he has, He will bless others, if we pay the price as you did. I feel like I did when I first found salvation.

Yours Sincerely,
E.J.

Cobourg, Ontario, Canada.

Dear Sister Dabney:—

We are grateful for your letters. May God bless you. It is wonderful how God condescended and blessed your soul to pray. Your letters are powerful. A few prayer warriors and I observed the contents of your letter, then we shared it with others. My dear, the very presence of God touch our hearts. Will you come to us some day?

Yours in Christ,
E.T.

Brantford, Ontario, Canada.

Dear Sister:—

A friend of mind sent me a tract someone published concerning your experience in prayer. It is the sweetest story I have heard in a long time. It seemed so hard to pray a few minutes today, and just to think God has blessed you to pray continually. It is a miracle today. I trust you will answer this letter. It must be wonderful to walk with God as you do.

Lovingly yours in His service,
A.E.

Fairville, St. John, N.B., Canada.

Dear Sister Dabney:—

Since I heard you are interested in everybody I am writing to let you know I am a prayer warrior also. I want to know where did you find so much patience in this busy age to give all of your time to prayer. It is a wonderful life to live, but very few people are able to meet God in the way you have found Him. Write at once.

Yours in Christ,
H.K

TO MY CLASS NUMBER FOUR

When soldiers work hard on the battlefield,
They never have time to play.
They must go forward, they cannot yield,
They must toil both night and day.
They cannot stop when the bullets rain;
They must press the battle through.
Regardless what comes they must stand—
This reminds me, dear STAFF, of you.
You are always neat, sweet and fair,
You are tender, kind and true,
The life you live is one long prayer;
I adore the way you do.
You never come in after time,
You never take space to rest.
Although you may not receive a dime,
You try to do your best.
You are my helpers, the Lord sent you
To help me in a day like this.
You are honest, strong and brave, too.
You shall be crowned when He removes the mist.
Fight on, dear soldiers of the cross,
Fold, seal and stamp letters here;
Your work shall never suffer loss.
You shall rest when you enter there.
May God bless my class Number Four;
It is a wonderful sight to behold:
The Little Usher who opens the class room door
And leads this group to the fold.
The junior ushers, the church secretaries, belong to this class.
I pray for your victory way.
You are working before the harvest pass.
This is very essential today.
Now, soldiers, be wise, stay in your rank;
Be careful what you say;

The enemy is standing on the gangplank,
If you sin then you must pay.
Take time to consider how I am suffering for you.
How God has answered our prayers.
Be careful where you go, and what you do;
Remember He is everywhere.
Some feel sorry when caught in sin's alarm,
But this is not wise for you;
Do good, shun evil, keep away from wrong,
You must have forethought, too.
Give space for the aged to enjoy your life
Study your Bible if you want to do well,
Remember those who fail because of strife,
Watch the red lights where they fell.
Never grow too modern to pray,
Live right, this is your godly part.
Examine your life at the close of each day,
Consider what you have in your heart.
May this tribute I pay to you
Reveal a glorious scene.
You asked me why did I pray through,
Dear Children, this is what it means.

Dedicated to my brother, P. Jackson

When you and I were very small,
What mother said was true.
She said some day you would be called,
To help make things new.

You said you'd be a mechanic real,
You have proved this everywhere.
Regardless where you go in the mechanic field
You never have to fear.

I asked the Lord to call you to preach,
I see now it was not His will;
But He blessed your head and hands to teach
To revive the machines that are still.

Do you remember those days we used to play
Along the hillsides green?
You would sing, and I ran away.
Oh! This was a wonderful scene.

Do you remember how we used to creep,
Around the old chimney there.
And watch the tears stream down mother's cheeks
As she called our names in prayer?
Many changes have been made since then,
But regardless where you may be,
Remember God saves the souls from sin
And this included you and me.

We never had to live without
The prayer altar in our home;
You and I could never doubt
That the Comforter has come.

I know it never crossed your mind,
This day you would live to see;
The book I wrote during my prayer time,
And this poem I composed for thee.

Your dear little wife went day and night
Unto our mission there.
She always worked with all her might,
She loved to be in prayer.

When you grow old, tired and gray,
I trust this book will be
A token to encourage you along the way,
It is my prayer for thee.

Dedicated to Mr. and Mrs. Carrol Smith

You may not consider nor understand
The little things to be great you do.
You always obey the Lord's command,
You are humble and faithful, too.
There is no rest for a soldier like me;
My heart must be burdened down.
He made you like a merchant-ship on the sea,
You give me sunshine all the time.
Thank you for the flowers you give to me;
It is a pleasure to enter my room,
Jesus is pleased with your love to see,
It reminds me of the bride and groom.
Sometimes your kindness makes me cry,
It is a real spectacular view,
To think a hard working soldier as I
Has been remembered by friends like you.
You never mind the price you pay,
The best from the florist you request,
Over there you will reap some day,
When you become my Father's Guest.
You give me flowers before I go
Into that great heavenly land;
My task is great, but what want I more
Than to have you to understand,
My heart, my soul, prayed through; I am free.
I am a soldier who fought alone.
When you arrive over there, look for me,
Somewhere around His precious Throne.
The time has come, I must close my book
With this prayer dedicated to you;
Whenever your way seems dark, just look,
It will give you courage to go through.

My Father bless and undertake,
In everything we do.
Let your blood prevail and these fetters break.
Send us the morning dew,
Support us with Thy strong arm,
Oh! The mist is passing away,
Hide us from the enemies wrong,
In Jesus Name we pray.
Step by step forward we go,
Dear God, help us today;
Guide us safely to that shore,
Sail with us all the way.
Save your people, Saviour dear;
Fill their hearts with love sublime,
Deliver and cast away this fear,
Close this book with your power devine.

Amen.